# Vipassana Meditation
### and the
# Scientific Worldview

# Vipassana Meditation
## and the
# Scientific Worldview

### Second Edition
### Revised & With New Essays

Paul R. Fleischman, M.D.

Vipassana Research Publications

VIPASSANA RESEARCH PUBLICATIONS
*an imprint of*
Pariyatti Publishing
www.pariyatti.org

First Edition, 2009
Second Edition, 2020

ISBN: 978-1-681723-21-1 (Print)
ISBN: 978-1-681723-24-2 (PDF)
ISBN: 978-1-681723-22-8 (ePub)
ISBN: 978-1-681723-23-5 (Mobi)
Library of Congress Control Number: 2020939782

cover photos by Jeannine Henebry

# Contents

# Introduction

I wrote the essay, "Vipassana Meditation and the Scientific Worldview" in response to an assignment from Goenkaji that turned out to have a long trajectory.

This essay has already gone through a first edition, published by Pariyatti in the West, and reprinted by Vipassana Research Institute in India, and I have been asked to produce an updated, revised, and newly copyrighted version as of 2019. As part of this improved text, I would like to clarify the importance that Goenkaji placed upon linking Vipassana to the ethos of Western science. The manner in which he stimulated me to write this essay reveals the skillful means he used repeatedly to elevate Vipassana to the world stage. He pointed me towards writing this essay by turning me in a direction that gradually unfolded into it. By placing me in a position where I would become aware of the growing needs of the international Vipassana community, this essay became inevitable as the meeting point between the traditional presentation of meditation and the thought patterns of a changed, modern audience.

One of Goenkaji's talents was his skill identifying the abilities of his students that would make them proper agents to fulfill particular assignments. I have felt lucky to be appointed as a public speaker and writer on behalf of meditation. I have always understood that the heart of my assignment was not advertising, publicity, or salesmanship, but the creation of an explanation that describes Vipassana as an empirical and rational practice.

Goenkaji had a very strong volition to see Vipassana presented in the context of science. Throughout his ten-day discourses there is a constant attempt to integrate the Buddhist concept of kalapas, with the scientific concepts of atoms, and the concept of vibrations with the interchangeability of matter and energy. We all know that Goenkaji referred to Einstein and Galileo as Western icons who emblemized how we should assess reality based on reason and the universality of evidence-based discoveries.

My wife, Susan, and I first met Goenkaji in 1974 at a "gypsy course" (which is what he called non-Center courses in those days) in Mehrauli, at a Jain Ashram, almost within sight of the Qutub Minar, not far from New Delhi. Although Goenkaji was friendly and personable, he made it very clear that a Vipassana teacher was similar to a secular professional, in that he did not set up personal, family-style relationships with his students. By his deportment, Goenkaji showed that he was not intending to be either a guru, or an intimate friend, but that his role was limited to being a teacher, analogous to a professor.

It was in this way that we viewed our early years of relationship with Goenkaji, both in India, and later when he came to Canada, and then to Massachusetts. During the early courses in Massachusetts at the beginning of the1980s, in the hill town of Goshen and later on Cape Cod, he was an educator who we looked forward to seeing, but the focus of his discourses was on practicing Vipassana, and not upon the teacher's personality. To reinforce his image as someone who was not after either money or inappropriate relationships, he kept all his meetings with students short and to the point, even those meetings that occurred outside of the ten-day course time frame. He would not allow people to take photographs of him for fear that the photographs could become objects of devotion that might lure students away from actual meditation practice.

And so Goenkaji remained to us a benign but somewhat remote presence.

The first time that Goenkaji became important to me as a personality  was while I was sitting a long course at

Dhammagiri, probably around 1988, when I had already been appointed an assistant teacher, and I had doubts that I could fulfill the obligations that went along with this assignment. Early in the course, I went to see Goenkaji for a noon interview, and I told him that I wanted to resign from being an assistant teacher, because at that time I was a doctor, practicing psychiatry, the father of a small child, a family man, and also a writer, and I did not feel that I would be able to fulfill the obligations that went along with the AT responsibilities. I told Goenkaji that I did not imagine that I would be able to make adequate progress in Vipassana to justify my sitting on the Dhamma seat.

When I told this to Goenkaji he waved his hand in front of me, as if he were dispelling the aftereffects of my words, and he said, "Your progress in Dhamma has absolutely nothing to do with how many courses you sit, or how many long courses you sit, or how long your long courses are, or how many courses you conduct. Your progress in Dhamma has to do with the progress you have made in millions upon millions of lifetimes." I was shocked by the authoritative tone of his voice, and the radical content of his words. His thoughts did not derive from conventional worldviews. This episode alerted me to Goenkaji's expanded sense of time, and his understanding of the vast platform upon which Dhamma unfolds. This was the pebble that dropped into me, and started the ripples of recognition that Western cosmology and Goenkaji's understanding of Vipassana were set upon similar stages. This became the first nucleus of "Vipassana Meditation and the Scientific Worldview."

But there was another dimension behind the development of this essay, which was the issue about how to address the secular audiences of the Western world. First, as an AT, and then as an Acariya appointed to Dhamma outreach, I had to consider the role of skillful communication in teaching and spreading Dhamma.

In the late 1980s, when Goenkaji met with Susan and me as a newly appointed AT couple, who were checking on one of his large courses at the still raw tent site that was to become Dhamma Dhara, Massachusetts, he emphasized to us the importance of family life for Vipassana ATs. "Family comes first" was his motto, by which he meant that we should not short-change family in order to serve Dhamma, but that we should use all of our skillful means to gracefully fulfill both sets of obligations, without setting them up as competitors to each other. Goenkaji advised us about the importance for the spread of Dhamma in having people with families to serve as ATs, so that Vipassana would be understood through living example as a practice that was not limited to celibate people or to monastics. Goenkaji was eager to find meditator families who could become the living face of Dhamma, because, as he said, "Most of the world consists of married people in families. If we do not attract these people to Dhamma, we will not have served suffering humanity in our era." In other words, Goenkaji set a goal of expanding Vipassana practice beyond the boundaries of Asian monasticism where it had been sequestered for generations. This transformation necessitated not only new kinds of participants, but also new language skills.

While we were serving on one of Goenkaji's courses in Massachusetts, we had an educative experience listening to his noon interviews, which also subtly helped to set the stage for "Vipassana Meditation and the Scientific Worldview." Goenkaji seated us to the side of him, each of us facing the student from the angle of Goenkaji's right or left side, where he asked us to just sit still and listen, as is now done in Step 1 AT training. An old student came to Goenkaji and complained that she did not have time to take care of her family, and to serve also on ten-day courses. Goenkaji reassured her that family came first, that her role now was to be a mother, and that later in life she would have plenty of time to serve after her children had grown. But when another mother made a similar complaint, Goenkaji told her that she was just making an excuse to avoid Dhamma service, and that a person who did not understand the importance of service had not understood Vipassana. From these cases of apparently contradictory advice, we learned two things. Goenkaji had an intuitive, case-by-case feeling for individuals, and his advice was tailored to the person in front of him. We also learned why you can't quote advice from Goenkaji out of context from the situation in which the advice was given. His words were specific to the person and to the moment. This language precision he had about which student should be guided in which way made it clear that Goenkaji was honing his communication skills to reach Western students.

As the years unrolled, and Susan and I sat and served, and were ATs on his courses, Goenkaji became increasingly cordial, though he also retained his dignified remove. I remember how surprised I was, when I would visit him to pay respects as soon as I would arrive for a course at Dhammagiri, and his first words were always, "How are Susan and Forrest (our son)?" How could he keep so many people so clearly in mind? Later still, in the year 2000, he sent us a letter about our son, Forrest, in which Goenkaji emphasized two things: the importance he placed upon "high attainments in worldly spheres," and the central value he gave to "the most challenging, complicated, and delicate responsibility: that of parenting." Once again I was impressed by Goenkaji's reaching towards secular family values as the future location for Dhamma practice.

Goenkaji read all of my early writings like, "Why I Sit," "Healing the Healer," "Therapeutic Action…," relevant chapters in "Cultivating Inner Peace," etc. He was aware of, but did not read, my non-Vipassana psychiatric writing like, "The Healing Spirit." After Susan and I had served from approximately 1987–1998 as ATs, and based upon my writing and professional awards, Goenkaji appointed both of us to be Acariyas  serving Outreach to Professionals and Intellectuals in the West. We were lucky to  have a number of extended conversations with Goenkaji, at his house in Juhu, Bombay/Mumbai in the years after we were appointed, in which he specified how we were to go about fulfilling our unique but still ambiguous role, which he himself was still in the process of defining.

- The essence of our assignment was skillful use of language in writing and speaking to help Vipassana become a beacon in the West.
- Susan was to serve as first reader, listener, critic and editor. My author or public speaker's voice should always be attuned to the feminine as well as the masculine listener. Susan had pointed out to me many years earlier how careful Goenkaji was to use the pronouns "he or she" even during the era when "he" was still the convention.
- Goenakji assigned our focus audience to be professionals and intellectuals in the West, the group that constituted our natural niche, but we were also assigned to speak to public audiences when possible. Our center of activity was intended to be the Western world, not just our own locality. For our Dhamma service, we should not think of ourselves as located in Massachusetts, but as located in the West.
- Goenkaji admonished me to avoid acting like a salesman who needed to market a product. We shouldn't attempt to get people to come to Vipassana courses, but we should place information in front of prospective students for them to decide upon.
- We should use modern English enriched with the American idiom, the commonly used written and spoken patterns. It was the Buddha who had emphasized that Dhamma was always taught in local language and

dialect. At the same time, we were to think of our work as addressed to the English speaking world. (Subsequently, many of our articles have been translated into numerous other languages.)

- I should speak and write in my own voice. Having started his life as a Hindi poet and public speaker, Goenkaji was particularly sensitive to this point, that for writing to carry interest and conviction to other people, it has to stem from the signature qualities of individual personality. Every writer has a particular and unique manner of expression. Goenkaji was very emphatic that I should guard my writing against editorial confinement or intrusions. I should avoid repeating Goenkaji's manner of speaking, and should stick to my own natural spoken style. I should keep looking for audience-specific, changing sensibilities of time and place, rather than recycling any rote formula from audience to audience.

- We should conceptualize Dhamma so that it is meaningful in the West, emphasizing rationality, and freedom from beliefs or superstitions. We should persevere in creating a universal, experience-based presentation. Dhamma should not sound as if it were associated with any healing practice, or national culture. We should not promote Dhamma as being Indian but should explain that it is for all people.

- We should try to speak wherever we have been requested to do so, if at all possible. We should never impose ourselves upon anyone nor tell anyone that they should meditate. Meditation practice should always spring from a person's own volition.

- Goenkaji assigned us to build a bridge between Vipassana and science. Whenever possible, we were to explain the Buddha's compatibility with science. We should not blend Vipassana with psychiatry, which would blur the difference between a spiritual path and a psychiatric treatment. We should emphasize our confidence in the importance of psychiatric treatment where it is relevant, and we should not sound like blind believers, who recommend Vipassana as a way to deal with disease. Goenkaji reemphasized the importance of U Ba Khin's prescient insight that using Vipassana to heal mental illness would degrade the path to Nibbana into a subtype of medicine.

- We were to avoid debates, but we should feel free to speak where different traditions were being discussed cordially. We should address other Buddhist groups, and any other religion when we had been invited, so that we do not appear aloof, but we should avoid comparison or competition.

- We should not use exaggerated praise, nor hide limitations, such as the fact that not every suffering person will have the capacity to benefit from Vipassana. We should gain our audiences' trust with our honesty.

- In any audience, or in any group of readers, we should expect there to be fault-finders, whose tone of voice is marked by invalidation rather than honest difference of opinion. "Learn to ignore fault-finders!" Goenkaji repeated this phrase twice to us with emphasis, creating an indelible lifetime memory. We imagine he had his own experience with fault-finders. Goenkaji wanted to toughen us to face the many envious critics that he surmised we would encounter. (These conversations with Goenkaji occurred long before the internet and email amplified rancor.)

- We discussed "outreach" as consisting of articles, books, lectures, public speaking and audio recordings. All of our discussions with Goenkaji occurred before the explosion of internet visual communication like Facebook and YouTube.

- We should not lose our professional credibility nor our contact with audiences outside of Vipassana. When we were called upon to do so, we should retain our credibility as writers in scientific and psychiatric fields, independent of Vipassana.

This outreach assignment, with its public speaking and writing, placed me in contact with tens of thousands of people who were both interested in Vipassana, yet wary of its apparent foreignness. I was set onto the track of communicating about meditation in an increasingly data-driven secular world.

Over the last twenty years, we estimate we have given in the range of well over a hundred and fifty public talks around the world, predominantly in the USA, but also in Canada, Mexico, England, Belgium, Netherlands, Germany, Austria, Spain, Israel, South Africa, and even India, mostly at universities, but at many public forums as well. Audience size has varied from a few dozen, to five or six hundred. With an estimated average size of 150 people in the audience, over 150 talks would mean we have presented Vipassana live to well over 20,000 people. We have also written many chapters, articles, and books.

Almost all the talks that we have given have been framed as introductions to Vipassana, and the majority of these were presentations at American universities. After each talk we received written questions from the audience and Susan would select from the stack of questions those which were most relevant. In this way, we fell into a vigorous live dialogue with university audiences in scores of locales around the United States. Our living conversation occurred at Harvard, Yale, Brown, Tufts, MIT, U.Mass, Amherst, Smith, Barnard, Hampshire, University of Chicago, Northwestern, Columbia, New York University, Macalester, Emory, University of North Carolina, University of Washington, Evergreen State, University of British Columbia, University of Victoria, and many other places. Throughout this extensive exchange, the audiences pressed upon me their need to hear me address their widely held uncertainty as to whether Vipassana was truly compatible with the modern academic vision of reality.

But our audience was not merely the people sitting in the seats. Every talk we gave was the product of detailed orchestration, cooperation, and participation from many Dhamma servers. An important part of our conversation occurred among all of these committed meditators spangled across North America, Europe, and elsewhere.

Every pubic talk and university lecture became a celebration of Dhamma. In this way, we also learned about the importance of creating an understanding of Vipassana that is compatible with the lives of meditators who are functioning at high levels in the West. Our journey through so many public events taught us that there was a need for spoken, written, and audio material that was culturally sensitive to the Western students' demand to understand meditation through the lenses of university generated categories, like psychology, biology, or physics. We did not create the need to write an essay like "Vipassana Meditation and the Scientific Worldview." We recognized that it was being demanded of us.

A great deal of our written and audio material has benefitted from the existence of Pariyatti. We owe a special debt of gratitude to Rick Crutcher for founding Pariyatti, for stimulating us to write, and for extensive editing time. Pariyatti continues to serve as a site where we can post written and audio versions of talks that we give.

There was still one more set of circumstances that followed upon Goenkaji's assignment to us, and our writing and public speaking, and that was our advisory role regarding scientific psychiatry. I found myself writing about mental health in order to explain it to Goenkaji, and then to the teacher and assistant teacher community. This came about because, shortly after we were appointed as Assistant

Teachers and began conducting courses in the late 1980s, I realized that mental health screening was essential, and I began to promote this idea to Goenkaji, who was initially reluctant to turn anyone away from a Vipassana course, but who eventually accepted my viewpoints and became a strong advocate for mental health guidelines.

He wrote a personal letter to me in which he said, "I agree with your suggestion for notifying students in advance. We should not be shy to announce that we cannot serve everybody. Buddha said there are five requisites for practicing meditation and one of them is good health."

Goenkaji's letter to me showed his capacity to learn as well as his belief that he was not perfect and could benefit from the advice of his students. An important part of his leadership was his willingness to listen.

It took approximately fifteen years from Goenkaji's first acceptance of mental health screening for Vipassana courses, until his ultimate inclusion of the Mental Health Guidelines into the AT Kit. After that, it took another fifteen years or so for our workshops to educate the Dhamma community about the importance of mental health screening. Through these workshops in which I lectured, listened, answered questions, and exchanged teaching examples with many hundreds of assistant teachers, I began to experience another dimension to the scientific presentation of Vipassana.

The scientific worldview is not just information. It is an attitude. I felt that I was impelled to define science to a community of non-scientists in a manner that was authentic to the complexity of the enterprise, but that also made it comprehensible and useful to people whose lives had been pointed in a different direction. "Vipassana Meditation and the Scientific Worldview" began to flow through my thoughts as a set of sentences that I wished to say to my fellow ATs and Ts, as well as to the tens of thousands of people who listen to my talks. Many of them were trying to sort through the unique features of Vipassana in contrast to the proliferation of practices and claims that were beginning to show up in the West in the name of meditation. So it was through Goenkaji's volition and assignment to me, coupled with decades of public talks, and years of workshops presented to my friends and colleagues in Dhamma service, that the opening paragraphs of an essay on the nature of science began, clarifying what it is and what it isn't.

In my mind, therefore, the article, "Vipassana Meditation and the Scientific Worldview" is like a personal letter that I have written to my teacher on his behalf. It is like an email sent home by a traveler who has spent years on the road. Of all the books and articles I have written, this one comes closest to fulfilling what I feel Goenkaji wanted me to accomplish.

# Vipassana Meditation and the Scientific Worldview

**Dedicated to the Memory of S.N. Goenka**
**Revised July 9, 2019**

One of the important factors by which Mr. S.N. Goenka spread Vipassana meditation around the world in the second half of the twentieth century was by emphasizing similarities between the worldviews of Vipassana and science. For many meditation students this focus facilitated their willingness to give serious meditation a fair trial. For me, as for thousands of others, Goenkaji's reframing of Vipassana opened a door through which I could step out onto the Path. In honor of Goenkaji's educational mission, which has spanned the planet, I would like to portray the scientific worldview as it unfurled in the twentieth and twenty-first centuries, giving emphasis to the way that it can be understood to clarify such Pāli terms as *anicca*, *anattā*, *kamma*, and *Dhamma*. Science today not only highlights certain aspects of the Buddha's teaching, but it also adds impetus to the psychological and moral implications of meditation practice.

   To open this discussion I will define the scientific attitude and process. Then I will make a probe into those fields which substantiate and clarify core aspects of the Buddha's teaching, such as cosmology, physics, chemistry, biology, complexity, and information sciences.

   The Buddha defined awareness of the meaning of the rising and passing of body sensations as the meditative gateway to reality. For the meditator, the value of this experience rests upon actual practice. The world is revealed to him or her as an organization of complex, dynamic, and fluid compounds in ceaseless flux, following universal laws. This Vipassana experience is an immersion into the nature of reality that science has also revealed to us. By dipping into it the meditator can contact and receive wisdom from the Dhamma, which can be understood as the information state that guides the universe.

## A Definition of Science

Although science has become one of humanity's premiere occupations, it remains difficult to define. The scientific enterprise encompasses a large array of people, procedures, activities and attitudes. Eminent scientists often define science in different ways. Rather than a single, uniform entity, science is probably best defined as a collection of related and partially integrated events.

The simplest way to define science is the attempt to gather evidence which will disprove a belief. A commonly cited more formal definition is by philosopher Karl Popper, who called science the act of falsification. In other words, science seeks to show what is false about an idea. Murray Gell-Mann, who won the Nobel Prize in physics, put Popper's definition into colloquial speech: science is a sentence that can be disproven. According to Gell-Mann's concise definition, anything you say that can neither be proven nor disproven lies outside of the realm of scientific thought, and is just personal values. Science is a way of phrasing things, a way of thinking about life, that permits the possibility that what you just said can be disproven when it is critically examined. It is a way of organizing our ideas so that they can be vigorously assessed.

Popper and Gell-Mann's definitions are often described in scientific texts as the attempt to gather evidence to refute a pre-existing statement. A hypothesis is formulated; facts are elicited, assembled, and organized in such a way that they refute the hypothesis, or, failing to do so, add credence to the irrefutability of the hypothesis. If you can't prove it is wrong, then maybe it is right.

Despite widespread popular mythology to the contrary, science is not an enterprise of proofs and truths. It consists of ongoing exploration, working formulations, aggregation of data, and reformulations, without any final endpoint. It is a process, a lifelong attitude of reexamining what has just been said.

In particular areas of inquiry, accumulating evidence may become so powerfully convincing that further inquiry would appear unpromising for new conclusions, and this arena is then tentatively closed, "widely accepted," and colloquially said to be "proven." If you have tried many times to prove that a hypothesis is false, and it has recurrently been found to resist refutation, then it has gained credibility in a powerful way.

But as scientific history evolves, old "facts" are often overturned. As early as the eighteenth century, the philosopher, Immanuel Kant, set the tone for science when he defined it as moderation in our claims, and caution in our assertions. In other words, science can be thought of as living life with "organized skepticism," as it was called by Harvard philosopher of science, Robert Merton, that is to say, not random cynicism, but an organized effort to live according to rigorous standards of truth. The scientist is skeptical in an organized way, not capriciously, but relentlessly refusing to accept unsubstantiated statements or beliefs.

Because science rests upon human activities, sensory information that is used to record experimental evidence, and communication among scientists, it is subject to the errors that are potential within each of these realms. Its own methods contain ambiguities and uncertainties. So science is an attempt to disprove untruths by using methods that are pretty good, but that are not flawless. This does not mean science is flawed, but it does mean that science rests on inevitable and continuous tilting towards self-correction. The process of reexamining truth itself needs to be reexamined.

Scientific statements are continually refined, and can be understood to be the best ones currently available, but which nevertheless are only standing in line, awaiting modification. The scientific process has no endpoint. The scientific attitude is the assumption that if we look at our beliefs in the light of new information, we will probably need to change them.

Scientific inquiry is also focused on clarity and simplicity. Einstein famously described science as the rational unification of the manifold, making coherent sense out of many phenomena. Einstein also said that science was the search for the smallest possible number of conceptually independent elements. Many things get collected into simple rules, called the laws of science, which are then tested in order to withstand refutational challenges.

The outcome of science is simple ideas that account for complex phenomena. The best scientific hypothesis is the one that describes the most data in the most parsimonious way. This helps account for the important role that mathematics plays in science, because it can hold many ideas in brief symbols.

Because an unknown result by an isolated person does not enter into the scientific canon, science can also be understood as a conversation about observable outcomes, which are in the public domain, and which are published in written documents subject to examination. Science does not exist without conferences and journals in which people challenge each others' findings. Socially acceptable refutational arguments are necessary to the scientific enterprise.

On the other hand, because science only exists in the context of society, language, and discourse, culturally constructed beliefs may become subtly inserted in ways that are opaque to one generation and which may require modification or excision by subsequent generations. For example, prominent scientists in Nazi Germany continued to believe in racial inequality long after such ideas had been refuted by science. The culture of Nazi Germany encouraged the retention of ideas in the scientific community because those ideas were comforting to political and social elites. When particular blind beliefs are very widely accepted, or are reinforced by rule, law, or threat, these non-scientific ideas may nevertheless become embedded in and carried along in the stream of scientific thinking.

Even the topics that are chosen for examination may reveal cultural bias. Certain topics may be so taboo that scientists are afraid to study them. If the authorities are going to burn you alive at the stake for your organized skepticism, it is understandable if you choose to close your eyes to certain unscientific belief systems. Giordano Bruno was burned at the stake in 1600 by the Catholic church because he proposed that stars were distant suns surrounded by their own planets which might contain life, and that the universe is infinite. Even though Bruno's ideas predicted the conclusions of modern cosmology, it is understandable why no one championed his insights. Even as a scientist, you may choose to turn a blind eye to the cultural constructions of your historical era. The pure ideals of science can be distorted by social pressures.

Therefore, scientific progress also entails dramatic restatements and rearrangements of what had previously seemed definitive. These "paradigm shifts" also transform our culture, which rests so heavily on apparent conclusions from scientific study. While science may be modest in its claims towards final truths, it also must be bold in its thoughts, so that it does not remain embedded in a previous century's blinders, and retains the spirit necessary for daring refutations. Science builds civilizations, and also overturns them.

Science accumulates and preserves understanding from previous and contemporary findings, and is dependent upon books, libraries, and public meetings to archive this knowledge. The embedded and linked investigations can be said to form an edifice of tested statements. Science becomes a dense web of sentences that have withstood the attempts to overturn them, and which become woven resiliently into a multidimensional matrix of knowledge and information that permits better problem solving. The logically consistent, empirically tempered fabric of existing constructs makes the scientific worldview an invaluable resource for reality testing. It steers actions that are most likely to be consistent with their desired outcomes. Because of aggregated scientific data, societies can depend less upon superstitious beliefs, or propitiating nonexistent deities, and may design more reliable ways of defining and predicting events.

The scientific worldview is different from the modern deconstructionist attitude that all truth is relative because it always rests upon culturally constructed stories. Instead, science is an interlinked zone of  evidence, testing, conversation, organization, argument, and courage. It bears no resemblance to purely imaginative storytelling.

If science does not achieve final proof, then in the phrasing of nuclear physicist and philosopher Bernard d' Espagnat, science probes reality until it strikes something that says "No" to our assumptions. Insisting upon evidence makes us challenge and correct ourselves.

Although the history of science reveals a wobbling, rambling, excursion through varying renditions of perceived reality, it also comes to rest at last upon a deep-seated intellectual foundation. It measures how far we have distanced ourselves from credulity, from superstitious assumptions, from mistaking coincidence to be cause, from fantasy, wishful daydreaming, or cowering in front of authority. It is the attempt to know what is true by daring to ask the question, "How can you show me that what you just said is true?" It depends upon emotional maturity as much as upon evidence, since it requires the ability to extract oneself from the comfort of tradition. It is how we discovered the brain cell, the airplane, the internet, and the cosmos. If you like galaxies, thank a scientist.

Although science is limited by its time and place, it eventually breaks free of these constraints. Whatever your historical location, ethnicity, gender, or identity, when you hold a stone in your hand and let go of it, it falls down. Science starts with stories called hypotheses, and it can also be diverted and polluted by motivated disinformation, but in the long run it is not a collection of stories at all but an observation that stones fall down.

## Expanding Universe

Among the many moments that we might want to describe as a scientific revolution, the one that seems most shattering and rejuvenating to me is the work of astronomer Edwin Hubble, who, during the 1920s, working on Mt. Wilson, in southern California, first showed that the distant, hazy nebulae were actually other galaxies, and who went on to determine that the universe is expanding. Hubble can be said to have discovered the universe. Before him, the best and brightest, even Einstein, believed they lived in a single galaxy cosmos of fixed positions and dimensions. Hubble stretched our sense of space one thousand millionfold (it has grown a lot since then!), and revealed dynamism and change as properties of everything we see. Einstein nobly publicized his own errors and lauded the triumph of Hubble's vision. Hubble gave birth to scientific, observational cosmology out of the domain of astronomy.

If the universe is expanding rapidly and continuously, an inescapable conclusion seems to be that it was once a lot smaller. Extrapolating backward from Hubble's findings, cosmologists constructed the model for what has playfully been called The Big Bang, a universe that about fourteen billion years ago was small, compressed, very hot, and destined to expand. Also using information from particle accelerators and nuclear physics, scientists have created a description of the early universe that is so factually underpinned and convincing that it has no serious alternative hypothesis. Initially, due to unimaginable intensities of heat and compression, even atoms could not cohere, and nuclear matter and electrons existed in a diffuse "plasma." Over the equivalent of long human lifetimes but short cosmic time, expansion continued, the world cooled, and most of the visible matter of the universe associated into the simplest atoms, predominantly hydrogen. If you had to define the universe in a sentence, it might be: "Hydrogen atoms clumping together due to gravity." The clumps are the galaxies and stars, too many to count, too far to be seen. There are now thought to be hundreds of billions of stars in at least one hundred billion galaxies, stretching billions of trillions of miles away in every direction. Today cosmology uses other forms of electromagnetic radiation, similar to, but different from, visible light, such as microwave, and infrared, to "see" or contact distant, ancient or light-insensitive parts of the universe, and our sense of space has grown beyond Hubble's, and, as always, science is modifying its previous world view. In modern thought, along with the light-radiating visible stars in their galaxies, there are black holes, quasars, invisible "dark" matter, non-electromagnetic "dark" energy, and other discoveries and mysteries.

Of particular interest to meditators is the idea, embedded in The Big Bang, that the universe "began." This appears to be disjunctive with the teaching of the Buddha, who said, in the *Bhayabherava Sutta* of the *Majjhima Nikāya*, and elsewhere, that there are many very long cycles of world contraction and expansion. No scientists doubt that the current universe is expanding from a previously compressed state, but the idea that the Big Bang represents a beginning out of nowhere is far from the only tenable viewpoint held by scientists. Other theories include the idea of multiverses — many universes of which our time-space is just one — or of cyclic universes of expansion and contraction. Two very eminent cosmologists from Princeton and Cambridge, Paul Steinhardt and Neil Turok, posit an endless cycle of expansion and contraction, with similar huge time scales (trillions, not billions, of years) to those discussed by the Buddha.

As our universe expands and hydrogen clumps to form the galaxies and stars, the gravitational pressure within the stars causes atoms of hydrogen to fuse, and from these fusion reactions emerge two key developments. First, excess energy streams out in electromagnetic forms, like visible light, which is picked up here on planet Earth by plants, which capture this radiant energy and through the process of photosynthesis use it to build the molecules of life here on our planet. Second, as hydrogen fusion continues in the hot "furnaces" and "kitchens," as Carl Sagan called the stars, the rest of the chemical elements are formed. The iron in the core of earth, and the carbon atoms that form the backbones of all of the organic molecules which we call "life," were "cooked" in the stars.

Due to the vicissitudes of heat, pressure, and fuel depletion, stars eventually explode, or cool, or undergo other processes, like supernova that release their material into space. This stuff from stars may re-congeal into second-generation stars, like our sun, or into planets, like our solar system, or may remain scattered as particulate. Nobel Prize winning biologist Christian de Duve has described interstellar space, filled with stellar ash of carbon and other elements, as the ultimate source of life-material, "vital dust." With so many galaxies, containing so many stars, many of which have planets, mathematical probability compels us to believe that life almost certainly exists on numerous planets throughout the cosmos.

Modern scientific cosmology has awakened us to our location among vast spaces, many places, immeasurably large and potentially alive. Science has re-contextualized human life on coordinates of space and time that approximate infinity and eternity. The domestic and anthropocentric dimensions by which people had previously described the universe have been revised. While fine points of details may vary, we now recognize that we live in an echoing, ongoing cosmos, towards whose beginnings and endless dimensions the Buddha pointed two thousand five hundred years ago.

## Compounded Body

The human body is a remarkable compound. To truly understand ourselves, even at the conventional material level, we would have to utilize almost every field of science. Physics would tell us where the atoms of the elements in our bodies come from, and the basic laws by which they cohere. Chemistry could inform us about the combinatorial rules by which simple atoms associate into multi-atomic molecules. Biology would inform us about the origin and history of reproducing cellular life here on Earth. The evolution of life into the complex multicellular forms of which we are one is described by evolutionary biology. The development of mind, and of human culture, language, and societies is itself a multidisciplinary topic, involving anthropology, sociology, and other fields. We would need to consult them to understand how our bodies are sheltered, fed, and housed. When we introspectively scan our own bodies with neutral observation, as is done during Vipassana practice, we are peering with the lens of interiorception into the universe with all its matter and laws. We are probing into the base layer of all the sciences. We observe ourselves as compounds whose microcosmic location nevertheless mirrors the macrocosm. It takes the universe with all its materials and processes to form our bodies.

About half of the atoms in our bodies are hydrogen. Most of our body is water, and, as everyone remembers, water is $H_2O$, with two hydrogen atoms. In addition, hydrogen is found diffusely in almost all the big biological molecules of which we consist. We got that hydrogen from the Big Bang and its aftermath, the early cooling and expanding universe, when the hydrogen formed by congealing from plasma that was pre-atomic. Therefore, half of the atoms in our body are almost as old as the universe itself. Each one of us should celebrate his or her fourteen billionth birthday. Our grains are not only unthinkably ancient, they are peripatetic and widely traveled, having made excursions across light years and eons. They are only temporarily vacationing in our blood and bones. Although every person is a different size, and though no one can see so small or count so large, scientific estimates place the number of hydrogen atoms in our body at octillions, that is, 1,000,000,000,000,000,000,000,000,000. Even more remarkably, we don't lose or displace too many of them, a point I will return to when we consider why it is more common to misplace reading glasses or car keys than any one of our trove of hydrogen atoms.

There are many other atoms in our bodies, the remaining fifty percent consisting predominantly of common ordinary things like nitrogen, oxygen, sulphur, phosphorus, but preeminently carbon, which forms our branching matrix of complex and vital chemistry. Carbon is the element that is most adept at bonding to many other chemicals and in this way it is the key player in organic chemistry. Compared to our hydrogen, these other atoms are newcomers, mostly products of the star that preceded our sun, which blew up its star-stuff into the void maybe six billion years ago, long after the Big Bang, after which gravity reaggregated our sun and solar system out of the disbursed and floating ash.

In his book, *The Fifth Miracle*, physicist Paul Davies, who won the Templeton Prize for scientific discoveries about spirituality, has written that, since the amount of carbon on earth is finite, and since the number of carbon atoms within each one of us is so large, the recycling of carbon atoms into bodies, over the ages "…has some amazing implications. You are host to a billion or so atoms that once belonged to Jesus Christ, or Julius Caesar, or the Buddha, or the tree that the Buddha once sat beneath." Remember that one billion requires sextillion more to grow to octillion, so a billion atoms are actually only a vanishingly minute part of us. Our bodies are built out of Big Bang hydrogen, carbon from stellar kitchens, and residues of revelation. We are neither as unique nor as isolated as we sometimes feel. The great moments of the past are within us.  In the microcosm of our body, the pebbles of the universe are reconfigured. No wonder we are inspired to meditate when the Buddha is in our blood and bones.

In the warmth of our solar system, in the warmth of our planetary biosphere, in the warmth of our bodies, tiny things like atoms are subject to the jostling motions of heat due to juxtaposition and collision with their neighboring atoms. Everything that is ordered and regular within us must overcome the random thermal bumper cars of atomic activity which creates a subtle vibration of disorder and reordering within the basement of our being. Heat and motion constantly dissolve the order of the world and of our bodies. This tendency towards randomness, dissolution, and decay is called entropy, which many eminent scientists consider to be the most enduring and irrefutable scientific law. Entropy means that everything that has been put together will fall apart. The late Sir Arthur Stanley Eddington of Cambridge University, who has been called the greatest astrophysicist of the twentieth century, said entropy occupies the supreme position among the laws of nature. Albert Einstein said that the thermodynamic laws, from which the concept of entropy derives, are, "the only physical theory…which will never be toppled." It was in fact the Buddha who first placed entropy in such an emphatic position. His final admonition as he died, as recorded in the *Mahāparinibbana Sutta* of the *Digha Nikāya*, was, "All compounded things decay…"

Entropy, or the dissolution of all compounded structures, like our bodies, is also the quintessential observation that the Vipassana meditator makes as he or she introspectively observes body sensations. Every body sensation signals change, oscillation, decay. Entropy is also considered to be the basis of our sense of time. If not at a conscious level derived from meditation, then at least at a deep intuitive level, we experience ourselves as sliding downhill into disarray and decay, an inevitable destiny we can only partially and temporarily delay. A highly educated friend of mine once told me that the best laboratory for observing the cosmic inevitability of entropy is a teenager's room. He added, "The life of a parent of teenagers is a constant struggle against entropy."

The psychological intuition of the physical and cosmological reality of entropy forms the jumping off place for the worldview of both science and Vipassana. Both science and Vipassana place at the premier position the observation of transformation, dispersal and degeneration.

But where and how did the ordered workings of ourselves derive? If everything is winding down, how did it ever get wound up? In the section of this essay about information, when we consider how science describes "Dhamma," we will see how we have emerged as a standing eddy in the stream of time. We are temporary, compounded order in a world of entropy. Our ordered, reliable forms locally reduce entropy, while actually increasing it on the universal balance sheet. And not everything is compounded matter. Before we can understand the apparent contradiction between a universe in entropic decay which also contains many complex, ordered beings, we have to consider a number of other scientific issues.

# Enclosed Individual Life

Like the Buddha, Einstein considered humanity to be imprisoned in a delusion, an optical trick of mirrors, which produces a false picture of self. This false self derives from a misinterpretation about our apparent separation from the world. Inside our skin, we imagine, is "us"; outside is "other". In reality we are temporarily separate but fundamentally a transitory expression of the universe.

Life by definition uses enclosures called cells, which are compartments of semipermeable separation from the rest of the world. From bacteria to humans, all living beings are cellular (viruses are not complete cells, but they require the cells of other beings in order to complete their life cycle). Only within the partial safety and structure of cell membranes and walls can the complex chemistry of life evolve. Cellular life is vital, fluid, in constant communication and exchange with its environment. Life is a partial boundary that is always being crossed, and a temporary enclosure that always dissolves.

Although counting the number of cells in our bodies is impossible, scientists estimate that we contain between ten and a hundred trillion cells. If you started at birth, and lived to be eighty years old, and counted two numbers per second without sleeping or doing anything else, you wouldn't be able to count one one-hundredth of your own cells. We are much more complex than is generally appreciated. Since our cells are constantly dying and being replaced, some slowly, like brain and bone, some rapidly, like skin and blood, we manufacture an estimated quadrillion cells in one lifetime. This flurry of temporarily counter-entropic creation makes us a hubbub of sensational activity. Materials of old cells are being recycled. Energy and new materials arrive from our food, which must be broken down and retooled. Via the food we eat, new atoms in the clustered form of molecules are imported from the earth's library of materials, which are in turn borrowed from our old universe. Each one of our cells, and the combination of our trillions of cells constitute a vast construction project. And this seems to contradict the law of entropy, which says things are falling apart. So it becomes obvious that biology, the study of life, is a special phenomenon within the universe.

When we design new cells, it is always from the information contained in the DNA of previous cells. This story, generally referred to the 1953 Nobel Prize work of James Watson and Francis Crick, and roughly familiar to everyone, is actually the product of investigation by armies of chemists and biologists during decades of the twentieth century. Even as recently as 2009, the Nobel Prize continued to be about new discoveries affecting the chromosomes that hold DNA, and about cell division. Remembering that we start with one cell, containing DNA from both father and mother, and then replicate that in one quadrillion divisions, the integrity of human life is as amazing as the cosmos, which contains only its mere trillions of stars, for we are not only numerous, but also intricate and precise to a degree that we ourselves are challenged to comprehend. Since human DNA contains billions of messages, or information bits, science writer Matt Ridley estimates the human genome to be as large as eight hundred bibles. Since cell replications occur over so many years and so many times, you would think there would be a lot of errors. Why don't our ears turn into cauliflowers by mistake, and our fingers into squids, or, more likely, why don't we gradually morph, according to the laws of entropy, into cancerous, dissolving, decaying chemistry sets? Of course, we eventually do. But during the interval of our lifetime, we not only suffer billions of mutations, both from replication errors and also from environmental assaults, but we rectify the errors with corrective, proofreading chemical systems of incomprehensible precision and fidelity. Life seems to vigorously buck the tide of entropy.

Human life uses, preserves, and transmits information in our bodies at orders of magnitude greater than we have capacity to think about. During our lives, our bodies hum and buzz not only with thermal jostling and entropic decay, but with replication, construction, addition and repair. We make people out of cosmic atoms that were channeled by the earth's biosphere into plants, which we eat and then bio-transform into ourselves through nonstop, guided, highly accurate creation. The replication and creation of cell from cell is based upon a host of large, complex molecules, which accompany, guide, and fulfill the information within DNA. Ironically, the array of macromolecules, which are necessary for cellular replication, must themselves be replicated each time that the cell is. And in trillion-celled creatures like us, cell replication must also follow critical, unerring, tailoring, during which brain cells create more brain cells but no liver cells, or heart muscle cells produce more of themselves but not kidney cells. This differentiation into tissue specific cell type requires further detailed tooling. For every individual person, this entire process is read out from unique DNA, a person-specific bundle of traits that have traveled down the ages. Our *kamma* is ancient. Our DNA is like our own signet ring, our personal signature within the universe.

It is easy to see why a certain vanity of self-manifestation seems embedded into living beings. It is easy to see why we might come to overemphasize our creation rather than our entropic destiny. During its tenure, life is a proliferative activity without pause or stasis. When we meditate on body sensations, we experience, along with entropic jostling, "time's arrow," the quadrillions-fold frenzy of life in creation. Our body sensations derive from creation and destruction.

All of this change, by which atoms are rearranged into the molecules and cells of life, requires energy, which we get from solar hydrogen fusion. Hydrogen fusion is caused by gravitational pressure squishing together hydrogen atoms in the hot violent center of the sun. From the force of gravity, and from the insides of hydrogen atoms, light erupts. Plants capture the light and through photosynthesis turn it into their own living green cells. We get our energy by eating plants (or animals who ate plants). But exactly how do we turn the organic chemicals in plants into our own brains and toenails?

This complicated process requires taking apart plant-based chemicals, and constructing the molecules of ourselves, and this is why energy is required. For the construction project of making ourselves we acquire energy by passing high-energy electrons, like hot potatoes, down a chain of complex molecules that through evolutionary wizardry have developed the skill to take exact electrons and use them for energy. We experience this electron transfer every moment because we breathe. We import oxygen into our lungs and use this life giving molecule to complete the energy donating electron transporting process. Oxygen lets the electrons maximally release their energy to give us life.

As simplified as this description is, three features deserve our attention:

First, we are transformation, energy ruled by information. We are the movement of sunlight, and electrons in motion. We are energy flowing down chemical pathways. Our essence is energy, transformation, and change, energy from atoms and stars, change guided by information stored over billions of years into the libraries contained in DNA. We are passing electrons flowing through macromolecular chemistry. We are electromagnetic waves taken from the atoms of the sun. We are energy from the universe rearranged by eons of *kamma* into us.

Second, because our energy utilization requires oxygen, and because oxygen is not a native feature of earth, but is itself the creation of earlier and other forms of life, like blue-green algae, or trees, who know how to catch the solar photons and store their energy in chemicals, like chlorophyll, we ourselves are saprophytes, dependents. We suck the oxygen made by our ancestor and contemporary plants. We exist and thrive only under the life-made ocean of air. Like amoebas swimming in a drop of water, we are a part of the earth biosphere. Every moment of our lives we breathe in and out, in exchange of energy, atoms and molecules. We share with, and depend upon, other lives: exchange and change. All of life is our mother. As recipients of life's potential, reverence for life becomes self-evident, wise.

Third, our use of energy is entirely unlike the world of physics and chemistry, like fire, or thermonuclear reactions. In biology, in us, energy is parceled out in precise, discrete units, quantified, with attention to detail. Random, explosive, or ionized energies destroy us. For us, the energy we get by carrying electrons down chemical pathways always remains embedded in specific chemical bonds. By making or breaking these designated bonds, we store and release exact amounts of energy in exact times and places. And about how many of these quantified, chemical, energy reactions do we make and break? Millions per second per cell, in trillions of cells. Yes, there are quintillions or so of energy-exchanging chemical bonds made and broken in your body every second! We can say that the Pāli term *anicca* is firmly anchored in biology. The number of energy transformations within us defies comprehension. We can add that the dynamics of biology creates numbers that we can tabulate, but to which we cannot really relate. To "understand" the energetic, transformative nature of our bodies, we require a more direct experience than our cognitions. Generally, people experience themselves as existence, something solid, stuff. But when we self-observe continuously and realistically during Vipassana meditation, we experience rapidly oscillating sensations of life's incredible fluid dance.

# A Brief Look at "Mind"

A brief overview of the science of mind cannot easily be written because there is no generally agreed upon scientific hegemony regarding it.

The commonest view is that mind arises from the switches and connections in the railroad yard of the brain. The potential numbers of interactions that are provided by the neurons in the brain are impressive. Our brain cells are estimated to exist in the trillions, and because many of them are networked to multiple others, there are estimated to be quadrillions of possible combinations of cellular interactions available to brain function. Nevertheless, networked interactions of large numbers of events, though they may seem to account for cognition or memory, do not seem related to creativity, imagination, insight, or spiritual vision. Networks of neurons can easily be thought of as loci of storage, organization, or rearrangement. But can they synthesize, imagine, create? Networks can compute, but can they originate and invent?

Many theories of mind include, along with the biology of the brain, dimensions of physics that might account for the more numinous aspects of mental function. As Einstein reflected, why do our minds seem to have such deep and fundamental connections to the universe? Why do human creations, like mathematical formulas, seem to correspond so well to aspects of nature? Other great scientists have also puzzled about the apparent link between human thought and scientific regularities.

The Tamil-American astrophysicist, Dr. Subrahmanyan Chandrasekhar, winner of the 1983 Nobel Prize in physics, observed that the human mind appears to be not only intellectually and mathematically synchronized with deep layers of natural truths, but even aesthetically, we find revelations of natural law to be satisfying and "beautiful."

Dr. Chandrasekhar concluded that what we call "beauty," is often an expression of a universal "truth." He was implying that our brains are set up to feel good when they experience deep aspects of nature.

Intuition, or meditation, seem to bring us "in touch" with realities beyond thought. Our minds might be biologically adaptive, tools that help us function and survive as mammals, but our minds may also tap a more fundamental layer, knowledge about ultimate reality, and not just knowledge about how to cope. Is mind a product of life, or is mind a function of the world from which life emerged? Is mind a product of the neurological network of the brain, or is the brain a biological adaptation that was evolved to utilize a preexisting mind in the universe?

A number of prominent biologists, particularly those who study complexity, like Stuart Kauffman, Werner Loewenstein and Harold Morowitz, have tried to explain mind as a deeper structure that is organized and amplified by the brain, but which predates humans, or life, or Earth. They imply that mind is pre-biological, a function of the physical world. They take as their starting point the Pauli exclusion principle, which was discovered by physicist Wolfgang Pauli, who was nominated by Einstein for, and then got, the Nobel Prize.

Pauli, one of the elite leaders of quantum physics, asked why matter doesn't clump, smash and shatter upon itself. Why is matter so reliably structured? Why doesn't gravity make the universe into one giant compressed ball (or black hole)? Why don't the numerous electrons that are found in larger elements, like carbon, bang into each other, creating a universe of chaotic ionized plasma, rather than reliable atoms? Pauli pinpointed how electrons within atoms are exclusive. Despite the fact that electrons are not little things, but are complex waves or particles or probabilistic distributions of energy, they nevertheless have uniqueness.

Electrons have a "spin," a signature or fingerprint. Each electron not only seems to know its own identity, but also seems aware of other electrons. By uniqueness in energy level and spin, electrons maintain separation from each other, an exclusion principle within the deepest structure of matter that keeps things separate in their proper domain. There is a principle of separation in the universe so that subatomic particles can combine, retaining both their uniqueness and their relatedness.

Complexity theory biologists, like Kauffman, Loewenstein, and Morowitz, see in Pauli's exclusion principle "the root of the organization of the universe." Matter is intrinsically aware. Relationship – awareness of the "other" – is built into matter. There is an intrinsic coherence, wakefulness, connectedness in things. The human mind may not be a unique creation; instead, it may be an amplification of properties of mind that are intrinsic to protons, electrons and atoms. Matter knows something and is not mere stuff. Or so it may be. According to this viewpoint, "mind" may be a property of the Big Bang.

The Buddha taught that mind is independent from, but mingles with and contacts matter. The combination of the two forms life. At the leading edge of science, theorists who have abandoned the brain-centered model of mind are catching up with him. For the Buddha, consciousness is multiple, and impersonal, a property of each sense organ's interaction with the external world. While we cannot say scientific confirmation exists for this, we can say that advanced biophysicists present us a way of looking at mind, and consciousness, that is impersonal, universal, independent from, and pre-existing any superimposed "self." We may be "aware" with down-loaded features of the universe. Though we may have generated its content, we may not be the owners of our mind itself. Mind may be a pervasive, lawful expression of contact between things. Morowitz has written "…entities show in their togetherness laws of behavior different from the laws that govern them in isolation…it is as if the second electron knew what state the first electron was in…a curious noetic character."

Johannes Kepler, the great astronomer who paved the way for Newton and the scientific revolution, may have had a similar idea when he said, in the early 1600s, "Geometry existed before the creation."

Because mind may well be located in relationship, in interaction, in connection, even within the context of the human body, mind needs to be reconsidered. The brain may be thought of as necessary, but not sufficient for, mind, which may also require sense organs, DNA information, circulating hormones and peptides, supportive cardiovascular function, in short, the whole person. The unique perceptivity of humanity may be based upon the complex connections we contain within all of our trillions of cells, of which brain cells may be exemplary but not exclusive. Our minds may be products of very large numbers of interactions of cells, atoms, body parts, and physical aspects of the universe to which our bodies are connected but which are not entirely within our bodies.

Deep sensations of mind, in contact with body, may utilize universal features of awareness. Mind may not be an interaction of brain and body, but contact of mind itself with every atom of the body. Mind may consist of an organismic integration of a whole mind contacting a whole body. Mind may not be located in one organ, like the brain, but may be a non-reducible function of the whole universe, with its matter and laws, compressed in a whole, integrated person. It may well be that in wholistic totality, and in penetrating detail, mind and body interact, from which our personal mind springs.

Vipassana Meditation practice reveals that mind has an interactive connection to the body, in its entirety, and in its detail. During meditation that is focused on body sensations, there is an opportunity to maximize the level of interaction between mind and body. Don't miss your toes.

## Beneath Matter and Energy

When Goenkaji taught Vipassana, he stated that the Buddha discovered that the world consisted of the oscillation of vibrations. What are vibrations? Is there a scientific way of expressing this colloquial word? Can the Buddha's discovery about the vibratory universe be linked up to the modern scientific worldview?

The Greeks thought matter and energy together formed the world. In his "miracle year" of 1905, Einstein wrote $E = mc^2$, and showed that matter could be converted to energy. Matter and energy are aspects of each other. What does the world actually consist of? What lies beneath, or between, matter and energy?

The world can in theory be unified, understood in the simplest and most complete way, by finding an ultimate building material, or a final and singular law. Science has not accomplished either of these goals of simplification and unification. Einstein spent decades searching for the unifying law, and could not do so. Murray Gell-Mann described the subatomic protons and neutrons as consisting of even smaller particles, which he mischievously dubbed "quarks," but today many forms and "flavors" of quarks are thought to exist alongside of other minute subatomic entities – a porridge rather than a diamond. A single particle, the Higgs boson, may give all other particles their mass, and like other aspects of the subatomic world, may exist as a field that can precipitate as a particle. String theory proposes that the world is built by entities that contain more dimensions than our human senses or thoughts normally interact with, but this theory is far from general scientific acceptance. Our best scientific thoughts, about the arising and vanishing matrix of the material universe, derive from quantum physics, and the standard model of particle physics, which was developed in the twentieth century by a pantheon of superheroes including Max Planck, Einstein, Niels Bohr, Werner Heisenberg, Wolfgang Pauli, Max Born, Paul Dirac, and Erwin Schrodiner.

When science explores the tiny things of which the universe is compounded, it finds a world different from the one about which our senses inform us. Our sense organs, and the logic that is built upon the information which they provide us, is useful, but not ultimately accurate. Concepts like "objects," "particles," "energy," "waves," must be jettisoned. They are merely gross, utilitarian approximations. Light, for example behaves like both a wave (light wave) and a stream of particles (photons). Things, like electrons, are less like tiny discrete particles, and more like clouds of varying density, locales where they are more or less likely to be encountered.

The bedrock of the universe seems probabilistic. Events, entities and laws are probable or improbable, rather than existent or nonexistent. There is a large degree of lawfulness, predictability, and order in the way that the tiny stuff of the subatomic world behaves, but also a degree of unpredictability and fluidity. Einstein made a famous agonized protest against this more relativistic quantum science, of which he himself had been the pioneer, but which he ultimately rejected. He exclaimed, "The Old One does not play dice." Einstein could not accept a universe that was ultimately indeterminate. But today, the scientific vision of the world leaves little doubt that the world's base is oscillatory rather than static, fluid rather than fixed, creative rather than stuck. Change and opportunity seem built into the finest level of matter, energy, and law. Matter is fundamentally energy, motile, oscillatory, smeared out in clouds rather than embedded in hard balls.

That explains how something that we think of as solid and clunky, like matter, can be built up from elusive fields, waves, and ghost-like particles such as neutrinos, bosons, and their fleeting subatomic kin.

There is a famous saying that, if you think you understand quantum physics, then you don't. We shouldn't feel smug when we notice how the description of the quantum physical world seems to echo the Buddha's description of reality. Quantum physics requires a lifetime of mathematical penetration, and its conclusions remain subject to change and reinterpretation. There has been a trend in popular science writing to give facile confirmation to philosophy derived from Buddhist schools by invoking partly understood discoveries of quantum physics.

For example, popular science writing has attempted to use the phenomenon of "quantum entanglement" to prove that "the world is one." In "quantum entanglement," under highly specific experimental conditions, two "particles" born from the same accelerator, seem to communicate instantaneously, faster than the speed of light. The particles seem "entangled," or unified across space and time. These experiments seem to imply that two entities that are separate can be under each other's mutual influence without any action occurring within time. Einstein argued that such "spooky action at a distance" was merely an artifact of experimental error, but, as the twentieth century progressed, unimpeachable scientists at CERN in Europe, and elsewhere, like Alain Aspect, John Bell, and Bernard d'Espagnat have created both experiments and theory that lend credence to the idea that in some deep structure of reality, apparently separate events may be "entangled" or connected. But these specific experimental phenomena, in very limited domains of applicability, hardly prove there is an underlying implicit wholeness influencing our lives.

Similarly, the idea that the whole universe exists microcosmically in a single atom overlooks the world-shaping power of interactions, which we have already seen in the exclusion principle, and which we will consider next. Many scientifically observable regularities, "laws of nature," are not found in every atom, nor in every grain of sand, but derive from the integrated interactions that emerge from contact.

While quantum physics itself remains unfinished, and provocative, rather than conclusive, we can comfortably accept that in his moment of revolutionary realization, due to practicing Vipassana, the Buddha entered a world of "vibrations". From our study of quantum physics, with its energy-matter interconversions, particle-wave duality, smeared-out probabilistic electrons, distantly resonating electrons, recedingly minute and various quarks, muons, or bosons, we cannot claim to have expertise in the nuanced and receding corridors of the ultimate. But we can follow the Buddha's meditative, introspective methodology down to his remarkably simple, unifying, scientifically-compatible description, of the farthest we can go. If it is not a final conclusion, it is also not an unreasonable or "new-age" statement, to say that the material world consists of vibrations rising and passing away.

## "More is Different": Complexity

"More is different" was the title of an article that physics Nobel Prize winner Philip Anderson published in *Science* in 1972. It is often taken as the moment when complexity-theory hit the scientific front page, providing a potential way of thinking about how an impersonal, law-bound universe could create thinking, feeling, human beings.

The universe is a self-interacting system. Its components encounter and influence each other. Forces like gravity clump matter; matter engages with itself according to the laws of physics and chemistry. Stars are drawn into being by gravity clumping cosmic dust; compounds, molecules, living beings emerge on our planet, resonating, as we have seen, with vast numbers of interactional events. In our own bodies alone, the number and variety of interactions defies our computational understanding. So it is very obvious that the world is complicated, that the universe and its life forms arose from richly interactive events. But complexity theory carries us further.

Within the context of innumerable interactions that form our body, or that animate the world, the complexity of the systems may not be merely additive. The greater the number of atoms and lawful regularities involved, the greater the complexity, true; but complexity often appears to increase in another, faster way, as if events did not merely add to events, but multiplied each other, or amplified the system in exponential growth of complexity, or, most importantly, engendered creative leaps into entirely different domains of highly complex new realities. More events, and more interactions, do not just drive more events and interactions of a similar nature. More events and interactions create entirely different phenomena. The universe contains scientific laws that emerge at new levels of complexity. These new laws either were unobservable, or possibly did not even exist, until the self-interacting universe created so many engagements of thing upon thing that entirely new aspects of reality became apparent. The universe exfoliates out of itself, gradually expressing new potential arrangements of matter and energy that are radically different from those which could be observed at lower levels of complexity. The world is less like a stepladder, more like an upward spiral. It appears to be able to break out from its previous symmetries into asymmetrical originality.

There has been an enduring debate between determinists, like Einstein, who believed that every event is caused, and those who believe in free will, which makes a space in the universe for events that are not predetermined. Complexity theory forges a middle path. The universe does not violate its intrinsic lawfulness, but the lawfulness engenders such complex phenomena, like human beings, like the human mind and will, that lawfulness can give birth to creativity and freedom. Freedom is a steam arising above the cauldron of determinism. The quadrillions of synapses in the human brain, as well as the other potential forms of communication in the embodied mind, like circulating hormones and peptides, as well as a possible role for quantum events like exclusion and entanglement, within the context of the mind, create a system of such high order potential, that insight, realizations, options and choices may arise out of the jillions of vibratory interactions. The mind is the lawful universe at a high exponential power.

In Anderson's view, at each order of complexity, entirely new phenomena emerge. We cannot study atoms, molecules, and cells, and claim to understand life, or mind. Higher order events, life and mind, do not violate the universe's laws, but they cannot be reduced to the laws of physics, chemistry, or even cell biology, because, as their complexity increases, new universal laws emerge as part of that complexity. Life and mind express laws that are consistent with, but much more complex than, physics and chemistry. In humanity (even in amoebas) something new and different has emerged, following emergent lawfulness, whose sweep of rapidly integrated, uncountable interactions may permit insight, choice and freedom to become manifest in the universe.

Complexity theory permits an integrated worldview that contains causality and creation. This view echoes two aspects of Vipassana: the explanations of cause in the *Abhidhamma*, and the Buddha's emphasis that we create ourselves.

For human beings, across millions of lifetimes (or even across fifteen minutes) there are so many thoughts and emotions, so many volitions, that no single cause ever entirely constitutes the mind (until it is totally purified). Instead, as we read in the *Comprehensive Manual of Abhidhamma*, "there is always a collection of conditions giving rise to a collection of effects." Multi-causality and complexity dominate our human nature, and also offer multiple opportunities. Through the very long bead chain of mind moments, we follow the deterministic pressures of cause, leading to effect, leading to a new cause. We also contain the creative potential of complex multi-causality, in which so many causes impinge upon each other that no line can be traced between any cause and any one effect, and the froth of free will arises. In this way we can be said to cause ourselves. We are our own father and mother, as the Buddha phrases it. We are the hydrogen of the Big Bang, and the carbon of the last supernova, but we are more, and therefore different. We cannot be reduced to any single previous antecedent.

There need be no "soul" or "world soul" floating in some disembodied realm exempt from scientific law, to explain our suffering and our Path of freedom away from suffering. Instead, using scientific language, we can say that we are highly complex, integrated, lawful, impersonal, emergent phenomena. The order of complexity within us is such that self-observation can arise. Self-observation triggers insight into ourselves as karmic bundles of iterations of universal cause and effect. Insight triggers the capacity to optimize self-creation through right understanding and right action. We are complex systems, built on universal law, who can observe, understand, and use the causality that caused us, to steer our future. The freedom to use insight to escape from suffering is not an exemption from the scientific universe, but is the highest expression of it.

When we are meditating, the pyramid of number-busting complexity of atomic interactions within a human being permits the emergence of a new set of phenomena and laws. The phenomena are insight, realization, and the factors of the Path. The Path emerges out of, and consists of, universal law. The impersonal universe lawfully creates the freedom that dwells in human beings.

## Informatic Universe

We are lucky to live in "The Information Age" which gives us a new integration of science with Dhamma.

Information dominated the era of history following World War II. Leo Szilard created the modern concept of information. He also was the physicist who, fleeing Europe, called to Einstein's attention the Nazi's plan to build nuclear explosive devices under the guidance of their Nobel Prize winning physics colleague, Werner Heisenberg. With Szilard's provocation, Einstein notified Franklin Roosevelt, who instantly commissioned the Manhattan Project. The formulation of the science of information theory was not independent from the dramas of human suffering.

But information theory, initially elaborated at Bell Laboratories, in New Jersey, by Claude Shannon, and by Einstein's Princeton colleague, Jon Von Neumann, and by Bertrand Russell's mathematical protégé, Norbert Weiner, has reshaped our understanding of the scientific enterprise itself. The universe does not consist of matter and energy, nor space and time, nor strings, superstrings, nor vibrations. The universe is the manifestation of information. We live in an informatic universe.

"Information" means selection criteria that limit choice. If you have information that New Delhi is north of Hyderabad, then you know that you must (are limited to) go south to get to Hyderabad from New Delhi. Information limits how electric currents can traverse a computer, and therefore what paths the electrons must, and cannot, take. The scientific laws, which guide the universe, are information. Gravity told Newton's apples that they must fall towards the earth. Evolution limits biological choices by selecting for adaptive ones, and can be understood as a source of information for life, about the necessary direction of its flow. Information is built into the universe in the sense that there are limits to what can happen and these limits are why there are subatomic particles, atoms, galaxies and planets.

Information is not in the universe, as if there were once a universe of caprice into which information had later been injected. No matter how far back we trace cosmic background microwave radiation from The Big Bang, or any other phenomena, we find scientific law, or information limiting or guiding what happened. The universe unfolded with information. As it evolved, its complex set of laws emerged. As we have seen, some laws, like quantum laws, only give probabilities and likelihood, while other laws, like gravity, appear deterministically ironclad. Pure randomness, if it exists, does so only within domains of law, and therefore is only local and partial lawlessness; that is, randomness is a constrained lawful variant permitted by prevailing law. Randomness provides a pool of variation for incorporation into the unfolding order and creation of the cosmos. The pervasive, unwavering, orchestrating natural information state of the universe is what the Buddha called, "Dhamma."

Our minds and bodies are built with complex nets of information that are located within the realms that we call physics, chemistry, and biology. The information net that holds us together was passed down through the history of the universe and now lives inside of us. DNA provides some of the information for our current bodies. DNA operates within us according to rules imposed upon it by chemistry law. All chemical bonds, including those that operate in DNA, use the electromagnetic plus and minus, by which atoms form larger molecules. The activity of atomic nuclei and electrons are the moving parts by which the great eight hundred bibles worth of DNA information within us operates. It takes all of the information contained in particle physics, cosmic expansion, biological evolution, to bring us into existence.

Within us is every universal law. It takes the universe to make a person. Within us is the strong nuclear force by which atomic nuclei cohere. Within us is the Pauli exclusion principle by which electrons maintain their identity. Within us are four billion years of stored up information bits in our DNA, which is simultaneously universal cosmic law, and uniquely individuated, person-specific karma. We move photons from solar energy down electron transport staircases, which are made of cellular macromolecules, using the information of the universe's physics and chemistry, to capture units of the sun's release of energy, and of information. Every bit of sunlight is a solar photon that enables us (if plants capture it, and if we eat the plant) to say, "yes" or "no" to a chemical pathway whose process helps to form us. By taking in food, we eat atoms of matter, energy of chemical bonds within molecules, and information about the way these things are organized.

It is the aggregation, interaction, and complex *organization* of cosmic regularities that we label "physics," "chemistry," "biology," etc., which place the octillions of atoms of which we consist in their precise functional places. The information state within us, the universal law, the Dhamma, locates these more-than-galactic numbers of atoms into slots that are minutely precise. Of course, information errors, mutations, or disease occur, but the fidelity of life processes is both vast in number and exquisite in calibration. Too bad we can't just hand over our car keys and cell phones to our internal master of ceremonies, the Dhamma.

The original realization of the informatic universe occurred under the Bodhi tree and was promulgated by the Buddha. Before him, the universe was typically misunderstood as being run by the capricious volitions of the gods. The

Buddha described a universe of natural law that guided the ultimate particles and vibrations of the material realm. The material world does not exist either by whim, nor by a "self." It is an information state, a compound of incalculable amounts of information. Humans can understand this information by reason, and can experience its processes within themselves through Vipassana meditation practice. On the minute scale it drives the arising and passing of our material constituents. On the large scale, it is the laws of karma by which a banyan seed, according to biological law, produces a banyan tree, or by which our species has evolved over the course of billions of years.

The Dhamma, the information state within the universe and within us, is the aggregated complexity of scientific law. When we persevere in observing it moment by moment, we pull alongside of it the way Einstein famously imagined himself traveling on a beam of light and thus came to insights about the laws of special relativity. In meditation, we can pull alongside of and observe the rising and passing of our body sensations as they follow universal law.

## Information and Entropy

Information means limitation and organization. Entropy means randomness and disarray. Thus we have to deal with the fact that there seems to be a contradiction between two descriptions of the world that derive from contemporary science. The world is informatic, Dhammic, lawfully following the limitations of cause and effect (sometimes deterministic, "tight cause," sometimes quantum probabilities). But the world is entropic, decaying, running from order to disorder, from compression to dispersal. The world is unwinding. We have seen that both operate in our bodies: we uphold and maintain complex arrays of octillions of atoms, until we decay, accumulate errors and disease, and die.

Science answers this apparent contradiction between order and entropy in many ways. Some scientists believe that the universe, similar to a human body, is winding down towards death. Most scientists point out that high levels of order, like life on Earth, are small, local eddies of order, temporary circular flows of high-density information, sequestered in tiny corners of a vast, expanding, almost entirely empty universe, which consists predominantly of space devoid of matter or pattern at all. Stars, galaxies, and matter occupy a very small percent of the cosmos. In any case, life on Earth, taken as a whole, follows the laws of entropy, because it uses up energy and spews out waste – heat – which overall increases the total quantity of disorder in the world, while only temporarily increasing local order on Earth. (Global warming can be understood as one expression of expanding entropy secondary to the increased activity of life.) All of these explanations are based on the ideas that the information state of the universe is found only in matter itself, and that the universe began at the Big Bang and is subsequently expanding and winding down. However, there are other ways of integrating the apparently opposite processes of order and disorder.

We have also seen alternative hypotheses arise from twenty-first century science. The Big Bang may not be an origin but a phase. The information state of the universe, the Dhamma, has no origin, no end, does not "run out" as cosmic matter disaggregates and expands, because there are larger cycles involved (which might be better measured in trillions, not billions, of years) and because information is not the same as the matter in which the information manifests. Permanent information states may possibly exist and guide repeating cycles of expansion and contraction of the material universe.

Within our particular cycle of time, the information and vibrations interact, and complexify, through overlapping multitudes of contact between them. New degrees of order emerge. From simple things like carbon, water, and sunlight, life emerges, people emerge. All of this may only be part of a cycle that runs down through entropy, but then subsequently reemerges again.

Compounds like molecules and bodies are entropic. The information state of the universe is not entropic. The Buddha said that all compounded things are subject to decay. The Dhamma is not a compounded thing, and is not subject to decay. The Vipassana meditator watches with equanimity the arising and passing of their embodied sensations, and observes both entropy–the decay of all compounded things– and the guiding presence of Dhamma.

## Beyond Our Small Selves

The universe was not built for our personal comfort. It contains death and destruction. Its information can lead to atomic weapons on Earth and to engulfing supernovae explosions and black holes in the cosmos. But when we pull alongside of its Dhamma, ride along beside it, watching with equanimity its materials, its information, we experience its guidance. We can live according to our deepest meditation-derived insight into its implications. The information state of the universe, the Dhamma, manifests in materials but is not itself material. The Dhamma is the pathway from the physical, chemical, biological world, to the non-material.

Today we are lucky that the language and concepts of science encourage us to understand an unborn, unending, unoriginated, nonmaterial Dhamma to guide our traverse. The universe provides us information, which we can access directly through meditative, nonreactive self-observation, which awakens insights by which we can know who we are and who we aren't. We are products of universal truths, and we do not contain abiding self identity.

Vipassana meditation is observation of sensations without reaction. There is no one sending the signal of Dhamma but there is a signal. There is no one hearing the signal, but it arrives. In the twenty-first century, it is science, not mysticism, to recognize that we are products of a cosmic information-state that can guide us beyond our own small selves.

# Meditation, Science, and Religion

## Introduction

Is meditation scientific, religious, neither or both? In this article I will describe meditation as the conscious cultivation of natural biological and psychological processes that evolved to optimize our well-being. Because meditation may enhance some of our cognitive and emotional capacities, it may make a contribution to religious and scientific enterprises, but meditation itself is a secular activity that can stand independently from religion. However, meditation achieves its full expression by affiliating with some of the same social and psychological capacities that religion also harnesses.

Although meditation today is practiced in many nonsectarian formats, the origins of meditation are closely aligned with religion, and more particularly, with early Indian religion. In the twentieth and twenty-first centuries, meditation spread around the world as a method by which religious, secular, and scientific people could seek through darkness and light to find ameliorating wisdom.

## Meditation in the Context of Religion

Religion is an inexact word, that applies more or less to beliefs and practices that are intended to answer in a comforting way the great unanswerable, existential questions. Religions create stories that bring human dimensions to our attempt to grapple with otherwise dimensionless time and space. Religious stories personalize the universe. Instead of feeling that we live in the context of unknown, uncaring, or incomprehensible origins, religions provide their followers narratives about the universe, its founding, and its meaning, and these narratives become familiar and soothing because they contain a personality, an image of someone with human-like motives and emotions, who either has created the universe, that is to say a god, or who has defined a reliable way to flourish, like an enlightened savior.

Religious believers can participate in stories that answer the question of what life is, and how best to live it. So religions are not only narratives, but also prescriptions. Religions dictate behaviors that guide their adherents. Often, the prescribed behaviors are rituals that are intended to provide a feeling of control over uncertain future outcomes. Religions also prescribe behaviors that are intended to placate and mollify their followers' anguish, loss, and fear that so often accompany mundane life. Religions may instruct their participants to pray or meditate as methods of finding security or peace, placing their prescriptions in the context of a mythic history and a recognizable community of fellow adherents. Religions embed the individual participant within self-justifying psychological spheres of belief, practice, and community.

Religions generally contain explanations of the origin and justification of their story, meaning that they contain a story about their story. Religious myth and narrative generally contain self-referential insistence that their stories are unique and unimpeachable, based upon sources that cannot be questioned, such as direct dictation of scripture from a god to a prophet, or such as directly conveyed wisdom from a semidivine mythic hero who had attained full enlightenment about the meaning and purpose of life. Stories about their own origins and validity make religious fables circularly emphatic, because their truthfulness is attributed to stories that are told within the master story. Religious scriptures claim validity based on aspects of their narratives that derive from transcendent origins.

Anger often enters the interface between different religions, or between religions and the secular world, because religious stories are culture-based and non-evidentiary, and it is impossible for them to substantiate their urgently believed narratives about ancient times and unwitnessed discoveries. So religious authority not only rests on scriptures and rituals, but it also becomes embedded in vehement attestation. In order to affirm that their belief system is more than a fabrication, religious adherents need to devalue the validity of alternative or conflicting stories.

The more a story is asserted by individuals and by groups, the more it sounds credible to those who listen to it repeatedly from childhood onwards, and who come to feel that this story is the prevailing, unquestionable, only acceptable description of truth. Repetition of the story, and social confirmation of it by one believer to another across the generations, makes the story feel sanctified by both familiarity and by widespread assent. The cognitive biases of recognizability, peer confirmation, and the soothing feelings that accompany membership and belonging via participation in shared belief, all have the power to make fables feel like facts. The comfort and the psychological security that religious stories provide also means that anything which disrupts these stories may become subject to attack. When group securities are threatened, human communities often become angry or violent in order to maintain the primacy of their beliefs. The non-evidentiary nature of religions often makes them epicenters of conflict against other narratives or cultural groups.

As we will see in more detail, meditation can provide some of the comforts that religious narratives provide, but with the added confidence of direct personal experience obtained through participation in practices that stimulate immediate psychological and somatic feedback. Meditation produces confidence through experience rather than through belief. The ease that meditation may bring to its practitioners may give them some relief from the need to believe something, and may accordingly diminish their predisposition to vehemence and anger.

## Meditation in the Context of Science

Science is a newer activity than meditation or religion, and as a widespread social value and widely practiced activity is only hundreds of years old. Like religion or meditation, there is no exact definition for science. We can say that science refers to the creation of an explanation about how some feature of the world works, a hypothesis, and then evidence is collected to try to refute the tentative explanation. It is often forgotten, even today at the height of the scientific revolution, that science is predominantly refutation, the activity of discrediting false claims by collecting evidence showing that the claim is wrong. In its classical form, science is less involved with asserting a narrative than in refuting unsubstantiated assumptions. Because of this, science is less involved than religion in creating seamless explanatory networks of stories. Science is an attitude, an inability to believe in anything that has not withstood multiple evidence-based attempts at refutation, a position of "organized skepticism" in confrontation with credulity and acquiescence. Science is summarized by the attitude, "How can you show me that what you just said is true?"

Because there are an infinite number of scientific hypotheses that can be generated, because there are many ways to collect data about them, and because differing amounts and kinds of data can be collected, science is a never ending exploratory process and attitude. Science is built upon a self-critique, an assumption that current assumptions may well require revision. It is intended to be discovery without closure.

At the same time, science is not geared to produce comfort or a well-synthesized wholistic story. It grows piecemeal, refuting parochial and superstitious beliefs but not necessarily asserting the meaning of life or the wise way to live it. Evidence-based refutation of blind belief is the core practice of the scientific lifestyle, and it is available only to an elite group of educated people. Because it is not soothing or easy to practice, science's powerful arguments, based upon evidence, are nevertheless not widely acceptable to people who wish for more clarity, guidance, and self-assurance. The scientific attitude does not provide the comfort that comes along with the false convictions of unexaminable beliefs, and it requires a level of psychological development in which ambiguity and uncertainty remain tolerable.

Meditation and science grew from different branches of the tree of knowledge, but they have recently entwined. The autonomy of meditation practice, and its ability to often disassemble false religious narratives through its own evidentiary process of personal experience, has placed meditation in alignment with science. Meditation and science both embrace experience and evidence.

However, this alignment is not the same thing as an identity between them. Scientific evidence is collected in a public domain that can be confirmed by other investigators, and that rests upon measurable standards. In distinction, the evidence that meditation collects is personal, internal, unavailable for confirmation by others, and without measurable assessment standards. Of course, there can be scientific studies of meditation practitioners, and in these studies science and meditation may mingle in the same pool. But a scientist cannot be satisfied by insistent affirmations made by meditators about the nature of their practice, and meditators do not have to wait for scientific evidence in order to benefit from their personal experiences.

## Science and Religion

Unlike the kinship shared by meditation and science, science and religion have strong affiliations but counter-polarities. Both seek to improve human life, and both guide people to wonder about the great questions as to whether life has any meaning, any right path to live by, and any coherent origin and endpoint amidst an eternity of cosmic dimensions. But because science is the activity of refuting unsubstantiated hypotheses, and because religion is adherence to traditional stories, the two ways of understanding have often been at odds. Religions have frequently attacked science, but scientists have never banded together to ban religious texts or to burn priests alive at the stake. So we can say that science has forged ahead, in spite of religious opposition, and has often brought religion along behind it in its slipstream.

Science has successfully toppled many parochial beliefs and practices. The social sciences, that try to scientifically study past and contemporary cultures and civilizations, revealed how religious stories coexisted in numerous mutually inconsistent and contradictory forms. Studies about the history of religions showed them to be historically dateable, culturally local creations. Their claims for transcendent origins were actually historically regional claims.

At the same time, science and religion both guide the human spirit towards the sense of wonder, and towards the humility and reverence that cosmic contemplation brings into the human heart. Science and religion are often partners in stimulating the great spiritual-emotional complexes that seem to be built into human nature, such as reverence, gratitude, and spiritual love.

There are many quotes attributed to Einstein which were originally intended to reveal his unique synthesis of science and cosmic religious feeling. Unfortunately, these quotes have often been misused to imply that Einstein gave his blessing to conventional organized religions. If we consider these quotes with an open mind, we will see that they are his attempt to hold in one embrace the inspiration behind scientific inquiry, and cosmic religious feeling, but they are antithetical to conventional beliefs and rituals. These quotes cannot be accurately used to claim that Einstein said that science and religion are similar. Here are some of the Einstein quotes upon which these attributions are based:

"Science without religion is lame…Certain it is that a conviction, akin to religious feeling, of the rationality and intelligibility of the world lies behind all scientific work of a higher order…This firm belief, a belief bound with a deep feeling, in a superior mind that reveals itself in the world of experience, represents my conception of God…The cosmic religious sense…does not involve an anthropomorphic idea of God. It shows the nobility and marvelous order which are revealed in nature and the world of thought…The religious geniuses of all times have been distinguished by this cosmic religious sense, which recognized neither dogmas nor God made in Man's image…Consequently there cannot be a church whose chief doctrines are based on the cosmic, religious experience. It comes about, therefore that we find precisely among the heretics of all ages, men who were inspired by the highest religious experience."

The difference between a person who has grounded him or herself in science, as opposed to a person who has grounded himself or herself in belief, is that the scientifically minded person has the psychological security to live with an attitude in which uncertainty is never fully erasable, and in which certainty does not exist. Einstein's conviction that the universe is lawful was not the same thing as a self-righteous proclamation that he now has fully understood and can speak on behalf of all these laws. The belief in a lawful universe is a spur onward to seek more evidence, and not a satisfied rejection of the evidence-seeking attitude.

Since Einstein's time, science has been influenced by quantum theories, which understand the world to consist of oscillations, probabilities, and indeterminacies. As we have gained more empirical insights into subatomic and trans-galactic realms, humans have created narratives about the universe that are impersonal, and indefinable, less like religion and more like both Einstein's "cosmic religious sense" and meditation experiences.

The common ground of science, religion, and spirituality is found in feelings that they stir in people. It may be, that inside of us there is a mirror, a locus of knowing, that has gained adaptive value and thereby been preserved through human evolution, that gives our deepest intuitions and emotions an open door to cosmic secrets that defy narratives and even evidence. Deep truths may be most accessible in our hearts.

## Meditation in the Context of Science and Religion

Like religion and science, meditation is a general noun that does not have an exact domain. In common speech, meditation refers to quiet, internally directed, self-initiated, self-practiced, self-reflections. Meditation usually provides a concentrative focus by which a practitioner can sit still, reducing sensory connections to the outside world, and increasing self-awareness of body and mind. Typically the concentrative focus is prescribed with some authority, which gives the practitioner confidence in the historical or even the cosmic validity of this particular concentrative focus.

When people concentrate they become calmer. The calming effect of concentration can produce negative outcomes, like the hypnotic obsession that modern people have with cell phones, but this link between concentration and alleviation of anxiety was harnessed by ancient meditative practices, which intuitively grasped the fact that activating the prefrontal cortex of the brain in the act of concentration reduced neurological stimulation in the amygdala and limbic system, which are activated during upsetting emotions.

Because meditative concentration can only be achieved by most people for a limited period of time, most meditations give leeway to the paradox that meditation also traverses un-concentrated mental states, filled with daydreaming, memories, hopes, fears, and emotions. Therefore, most meditations are broadly based practices that provide their practitioners with biologically based comfort, and also with expanded self-knowledge, and increased skill at remaining calm, peaceful, and self-accepting in the presence of the kaleidoscope of biological and psychological events that dance in the meditator's mind and body as he or she remains still and self-observing.

The activity of retaining mental poise during a process that permits the mind to expand into all its potential directions, is a meditative balancing act that reproduces the essential activity at the heart of life. Although life retains a fundamental mystery about its origin, and about its existence throughout the cosmos, on other "Goldilocks planets," where the potential conditions would "be just right," and therefore allow life to evolve, we also know very clearly that life requires a temporary stability and order. The ability of life to keep itself relatively constant, within the confines of a boundary, is called homeostasis, and this is the essential feature that differentiates animate and inanimate existence. Meditation mirrors mental and somatic homeostasis.

Within our skin, we generate thousands of homeostatic processes that keep our bodies and minds relatively constant. We regulate towards constancy our temperature, blood pressure, thyroid levels, cellular enzymes, cell reproduction, cell death, and all the other innumerable processes studied by biologists. Life creates a temporary, ongoing partial stability, and an accompanying partial adaptational variability. We can keep our bodies relatively constant, and we can also transform our bodies and minds to respond to challenges. Our self transformations cannot disrupt our fundamental biological and psychological constancy. We can change and adapt only within a range.

Therefore, meditation can be understood as the intentional, learned skill of optimizing self-awareness and self-regulation of both the body and mind. In this way, meditation can facilitate better balance, self-restoration and preparedness for present and future flourishing. Meditation is the intentional practice of healthy rest, healthy preparedness, self-aware "eudaemonia," welfare or prosperity.

Because meditation produces well-being without ideation, or with relatively low levels of ideation, it easily coexists in social systems that are religious, secular, or scientific. Meditation befriends the comforting stories of religion, but does not require them. Meditation can retain cordiality with the unsettling refutations of scientific data collection. But meditation does not occur in a vacuum. Its homeostatic optimizations flourish best inside the context of friendship, because we are group mammals, and our natural regulatory processes require the presence of family, community, and fellow travelers.

Even meditators need to anchor themselves in historical narratives that connect them to the founders and practitioners who made meditation available to the current generation. Meditators benefit from historical stories. Meditation can be most fully appreciated when it is contextualized inside of narratives that accurately refer to its historical origins. But meditation communities, like all human communities, remain vulnerable to the narcissistic inflation of self-serving fairy tales that place one group of people in the center of the story of the universe that contains trillions of stars in billions of galaxies that have lasted billions of years.

Meditation ascends to its apex in the context of its own history and friendships. Its greatest blessings are the feelings that accompany it, such as love, and other spiritual emotions like equanimity and reverence. Therefore meditation can be redefined as the practice that leads to the endpoints of science and religion inside of the emotional lives of individual people. These endpoints are moods and feelings. Meditation can be considered the cultivation of benign loving kindness as a guiding psychological state.

## Personal Comment

I started formal meditation practice in 1974 under the guidance of S.N. Goenka. From him, I learned Vipassana, the practice of focusing meditation upon the neutral, non-reactive, nonjudgmental awareness of body sensations as the underlying basis of mental states with their narcissistic cravings and aversions. I have tried to practice the equanimous observation of my sensations, and the equanimous recognition of the constructed nature of my personal self, under Goenkaji's exactly formulated methods, ever since 1974. This teaching and practice of Vipassana is historically validated through connection to the Buddha's teaching as preserved in the Pāli Canon, but is not riveted to Buddhist beliefs. I am not a Buddhist. The practice has led me forward towards improved equanimity, *metta* (loving-kindness), and free service to other people in the form of conducting courses that use Mr. Goenka's digital teaching files. I have also tried to contribute books, lectures, and workshops to define the cultural context within which this Vipassana tradition can continue into the future.

Our human constructions on the surface of this green Earth remain as fraught, violent, ebullient, and creative as ever. My life has contained the freedom to meditate because I have been given such an uncountably large stack of presents, gifts that enabled me to have food security, comfortable shelter, intellectual freedom, and safe social conditions, in which I could feel the well-being of community and wonder. It is only through solid social, political, and economic lifestyle, that larger swaths of humanity will gain the harmony that I have glimpsed. The opportunity to meditate derives from and stimulates the creation of a loving and grateful life. It is only through a very long chain of evolution, and historical beneficence, that an individual emerges from the cosmos and looks back upon it with recognition. I have been made possible.

# Vedanā and the Wisdom of Impermanence: We Are Precipitants Within the Experiments of the Universe

*This article was originally given as a talk at a symposium about the word, "vedanā." I explained vedanā from the standpoint of a practitioner of Vipassana meditation in the tradition of S.N. Goenka. The symposium was held at the Barre Center for Buddhist Studies on July 13–16, 2017. The talk then appeared as an article in a journal issue that covered all the papers in the symposium: Contemporary Buddhism 19 (1):102-112 (2018) published by Taylor & Francis Production, Oxfordshire, U.K. This reprinting here has minor edits.*

I would like to tell you about about the advantages that accrue to a particular interpretation of the word *vedanā*. I am going to talk with you as a person who meditates for both my personal benefit, and also as my social contribution to the world around me. I am not a Buddhist, I do not know Pāli, and I cannot claim any etymological authority regarding the interpretation of *vedanā* that I will be using in this talk. Instead, I will be describing *vedanā* as it was defined by my meditation teacher, Mr. S.N. Goenka, who taught Vipassana meditation based on the definition of *vedanā* as body sensations.

I have defined my talk today as an explanation of the benefits that this interpretation of *vedanā* brings to the secular meditator like myself.

Interpreting *vedanā* to mean body sensations has two advantages. First, it provides a meditation focus upon the direct experience of impermanence and change within one's own mind and body. This focus is a clear directive that most people can follow into sustained meditation practice. Second, it leads to a meditation experience that is fully integrated with the scientific world view. Interpreting *vedanā* as sensations, and making them and their changes the focus of meditative mindfulness, leads to an experience of reality in which all compounded things are aggregates of smaller things, all are subject to constant change, and all are impermanent. This is both the realization of Buddhist meditation and the data rich, multidisciplinary conclusion of the modern scientific world view.

To begin, let's start with a brief overview of how Vipassana is actually practiced.

When I practice Vipassana meditation as taught by Mr. Goenka, I try to focus my attention on all the sensations of my body, either observing specific parts of my body, such as my breath going in and out while passing and touching my nostrils; or observing multiple parts of my body, such as simultaneously observing my two hands and two feet; or scanning my body up and down; or simply observing the whole body all at once. Under all of these circumstances, I am trying to directly experience the sensations of my body. At one level, these sensations are a product of my environment, such as the temperature of my location, or are the product of my diet, such as whether a cheese pizza I ate two hours ago has triggered my lactose intolerance. The sensations of my body may also derive from physiological processes, such as the beating of my heart, or the heaving of my chest caused by respiration. All of these different kinds of sensations are certainly foci for my mindful awareness.

But at a deeper level, which is simultaneous to, and physically embedded within the physiological level, the sensations of my body are numerous, dynamic, infinitesimal cascades of much smaller changes that are occurring in the physical substrate of my being. Over a lifetime of meditating upon sensations, it is these sub-physiologic zones of *vedanā* that become increasingly contactable, and stimulate the more transformative realizations that Vipassana awakens.

I would like to guide you on a mental journey into the experience and realization of meditation on *vedanā* interpreted as body sensations. This journey will lead us from the vibrations of our bodies, that we may contact as we meditate, into emotionally and scientifically important realms of reality.

Let's go back to those deeper, sub-physiologic zones of sensations.

The subtle sensations of our bodies have many causes, more than can be scientifically named or understood. For our journey today, I will simplify certain collections of causes of subtle sensations, bundling them together. I will assume that the mind and body are so closely interconnected that thoughts cause body sensations, because thoughts require neurotransmitter flows that have a biological, chemical, and physical basis, and that body sensations can also trigger thoughts, such as when we feel hunger pangs, and then we think, "I am hungry". Our sensations and transformations occur at the bidirectional intersection of mind and body, where thoughts move molecules, and where body sensations trigger thoughts.

The subtle sensations that we can learn to contact in our bodies through long-term, sustained meditation, are caused by the numerous molecular transformations of which biology consists.

All the sensuousness or pain of our bodies, all the delight or turmoil of our minds, are transformations within the atomic, molecular substrate of the body. This is the ultimate truth about ourselves, that we can become attuned to, through our awareness of the ceaseless changes in the sensations that are the analogues of the fluid chemical and physical underpinning of our minds and bodies. The dynamism of our changing subtle sensations reflects the movements of the world.

Our bodies are collections of atoms, that are organized into molecules, that function in the activities of cells, that cohere to form tissues, which interrelate to create an organism. Our bodies are not solid, but are molecules suspended in realms of other molecules, all of which are undergoing continuous biotransformation. We are molecules aggregated and in constant flux. Nothing in the universe is static or free from fluctuation. Not a single atom in our bodies is standing still.

## Three Pathways Within Flux

Trying to give scientific language to this molecular flux, we need to describe three pathways. The first is the material of which we consist, like atoms. The second pathway is the energy that maintains and transforms the molecular aggregates. The third pathway is the information that organizes material and energy. Meditation on sensations provides us with direct experience of ourselves as temporarily cohering nodes of matter, energy, and information.

We can understand ourselves as consisting of very large collections of atoms. Of course, atoms are also collections of smaller subatomic particles such as electrons or protons, but for the moment let's first focus upon our bodies at the descriptive level of atomic aggregates. Depending upon our particular body size, and also depending to some degree upon the way we make our estimates, our body consists of approximately eight octillion atoms. (This was an estimate that was used by Carl Sagan.) Octillion is a number that is too big for us to comprehend. Even trillions are beyond our comprehension, since we live only for billions of seconds and never experience any units, time period, or pulse larger than the approximately five billion seconds that we live. We couldn't count to one trillion even if we did nothing else for every waking and sleeping second of our lives. But these unimaginably gigantic trillions are only one-thousandth of quadrillions which are only one-thousandth of quintillions, and so on. We consist of atomic aggregates too numerous for us to comprehend. We can tabulate these gigantic numbers, but we can't really assign meaning to them or relate to them emotionally.

This noncomprehensible, trans-cognitive nature of our own being is one of the reasons why we experience a sense of wonder about our life. Wonder is a way of encountering and holding in our thoughts and emotions wholes that exceed our cognitive capacity. (I have described these ideas in much more detail in my book, *Wonder: When and Why the World Appears Radiant*, Fleischman, P. R., 2013, Small Batch Books, Amherst, MA.)

These very large numbers of atoms of which we consist, and which we cannot comprehend, are an *underestimation* of the aggregates that form our material nature during our lifetime! Even if we ignore subatomic units, we all know that our atomic materials are constantly dying off, sloughing, disaggregating, and being resupplied by the atoms in our food. We have to keep editing, rebuilding and remodeling our continuously decaying physical bodies. The atoms that compose us at any one point in time are only a fraction of the atoms of which we consist throughout our lifetime. The number of atoms that we employ to build our dynamic but temporary physical selves is not really something we can understand. The numbers get very big.

Almost all the atoms that we consist of at any one point in time are organized into the larger units called molecules. Molecules vary in size from single atomic ions to gigantic molecules consisting of billions of atoms. The large collagen molecules in our fibrous tissue that give resilience and strength to our muscles and tendons may contain millions of atoms. We contain more sizes and kinds of molecules than can yet be enumerated through science. Our master molecules are the information containing DNA, consisting of many billions of atoms. Since we have trillions of cells, and every cell has DNA, we also have trillions of DNA molecules that contain many billions of atoms, so you can see immediately that just our DNA alone produces trans-calculable amounts of material made of atoms.

All of our octillions of atoms are put into place. We permit as few of them as possible to become dislocated, dangerous, free-floating radicals. Putting atoms into place in a DNA molecule (for example) means that two more pathways of existence beyond materiality have to be activated.

Remember that we are discussing the science of our bodies in order to understand body sensations, *vedanā*, and then to understand the value of meditating on *vedanā*.

Moving atoms to make molecules requires energy. Atoms are moved into place in our bodies through energetic biotransformation. The energy that rearranges atoms, and that makes molecules, enzymes, proteins, carbohydrates, cells, etc. comes from the food which had also supplied our material atoms. Food give us matter and energy.

The energy in our food is located in between the atoms of the stuff we have eaten. Suspended between the atoms of our food is energy, electromagnetic connections which we call chemical bonds. Atoms hold each other in place with electromagnetic energy, due to laws in the domains of physics and chemistry. Atoms cooperate and cohere into larger molecules due to the electromagnetic charges they embody. The electromagnetism in atoms in turn derives from the balances among the electrons and protons in the subatomic realm of matter. Atoms hold inside them, or convey around them electromagnetic energy. But for the purposes of our understanding today, as we focus on the atomic nature of our being, we find atoms cleaving to each other electromagnetically in food molecules, and we find atoms breaking apart and releasing electromagnetic energy, that then can be used to build new bonds to form new molecules in our bodies. This use of energy to create new bonds and new molecules is called biotransformation. Biotransformation is the basis of *vedanā*, body sensations. Molecules can break apart to form matter and energy for new molecules, or may break apart simply as decay, entropy. And new molecules are constantly being built from the materials of matter and energy. Our bodies are shimmering with sensations caused by transformations.

As our atoms electromagnetically cling to each other within molecules, or reaggregate into new organizations of atoms in new molecules, these processes are guided by information. Our bodies are atomic aggregates in transformations that require energy and that are guided by the information systems that lead to the organizations that we call "us." Most people most of the time tend to imagine themselves as constant and permanent. Human beings have a tendency to identify with the organized whirlpool of atoms that are spinning through our informatically arranged biotransformations at any one moment. We are actually processes.

The information in our DNA has been compiled over approximately four billion years of biological evolution. It tells atoms, molecules, and other parts of us how to become the living things that we are. DNA organizes the atoms, molecules, and cells into complex adaptive systems that we call "humans" or "wolves" or "oak trees." We are formed *in utero* mostly by the sequential information coded within the combination of our parents' DNA.

But, actually, deep inside the atoms that form the molecules of our bodies, is information from the realm we call physics, which contains information that is approximately fourteen billion years old. DNA is not the only source of information within us. Every single atom in the universe has information within it from the domain that we call "the laws of nature." Through the intra-atomic information, the subatomic particles (like electrons and protons) become lawful enough for atoms to get built up in the first place out of the smaller grains of the universe's matter. The atoms in turn allow lawful aggregation of the bigger domains of biology, baseball, and babies. We are partly products of our food, our thoughts and feelings, and also of the universe itself. The subtlest guidance of the universe is within us. We exist temporarily because there is some deep reliability within things. The aggregates in our bodies that bio-transform and generate *vedanā*, are built up from the matter, energy and laws of the universe. Our transformations and scintillations follow universal law books, the scriptures inscribed within atoms and evolution.

In recent years, as I have entered, or should I say "hit," my eighth decade, I often find some delay in my cognitive information retrieval systems, such as when I am trying to remember the name of the folksinger who wrote the Willie Nelson and Merle Haggard cover, "Pancho and Lefty." (By the way, for those of you who have retrieval problems, too, it's Townes Van Zandt.)  It sometimes takes my brain an extra moment, or five, for me to access some well-known cognitive information, such as the name of an old friend. "Oh, hi......Fred." But it is interesting to contemplate the fact that I have no trouble automatically and unconsciously retrieving information that is fourteen billion years old, in order for me to organize the physical chemistry comprising trillions of molecules and octillions of atoms that cohere in place to form my physical being. What a memory I have! Most of the information that guides our dynamic being is entirely unconscious, and beyond retrieval by our minds, which access only a thin skim of information. We are much more complicated and well-informed than we usually credit ourselves for being.

Not only information, ignorance is also a powerful force. It may well be the root of suffering, and it is often one of the roots of maladaptations in human societies and cultures. But information, not ignorance, is the source of life, and of the organization of atoms and energy into human beings. We cohere for a while because the universe is informatic, combinatorial, proliferative, and creative. The particles of matter combine according to laws, and expand to cover the globe in "…endless forms, most beautiful and most wonderful…" in Darwin's extraordinary and frequently quoted closing to *The Origin of Species*. Information has enabled the stars, galaxies, solar systems, and the evolution of life. We can aspire to "wisdom" because there is some analogue for it within the workings of the world. The universe may well be partly chaotic, but it certainly contains some predictability, order, and lawfulness. There is information about how to live, adapt, respond, and feel well and rightfully born. The wisdom we contact preexists. We are products of the lawful, combinatorial, creative universe.

We are discussing all of this because we are discussing body sensations, *vedanā*, which attest to the many changes that occur in our atomic, molecular, energetic, information guided, aggregated substrate that we label "us."

It is now obvious that we have no essence, or enduring self. We are precipitants within the experiments of the universe. We are localized nodes of cosmic processes that sift, collate and combine matter, energy, and information across light years and eons. Our bodies, and the earth on which we stand, are formed, and dissolve, according to universal law.

## How Body Sensations Are Created

Let's look more specifically at how matter, energy, and information function to create body sensations, or *vedanā*. So far we have derived our material and energy from our food. But let's take a look at how our food got matter and energy in the first place. To understand *vedanā* as a manifestation of the scientific universe, we have to expand our inquiry to the cosmos, to the ways in which matter and energy become captured by "us."

What we call "food" is organic molecules, derived from plant or animal matter, manufactured in living cells. These organic molecules all start when plants capture sunlight during photosynthesis. Photosynthesis is the sacred golden ring through which solar energy becomes utilizable by living systems like us, and like our biosphere on Earth. In this remarkable cosmic invention, photosynthesis, the energy of sunlight, packaged in photons, kicks up electrons in plant cells to a higher level of energy. The solar photons, which can be thought of as packets of energy, can be described as colliding with and accelerating the motion of specially adapted electrons within chemicals of the photosynthetic green plant cell. (The electron that is "hit" can be thought of as another moving packet of matter and energy that gets speeded up.) So, the photon adds energy to electrons in special parts of green, plant cells, which have now absorbed the energy of the sun.

The energy of the sun was once physical, but now it becomes alive. During photosynthesis, light becomes life.

The newly absorbed solar energy can be used to create electromagnetic chemical bonds between atoms to make bigger molecules. These chemical bonds hold the energy in our food. The green plant can now synthesize the mother molecule of life, sugar. From sugar molecules, plants build the rest of their organic molecules, which in turn are the origin of the biosphere. Everything that is green, furry, or feathered, waves in the wind, or flies and runs, does so with the energy of the sun, captured by electrons during photosynthesis and passed through sugar. The energy that moves molecules in our body and creates our *vedanā* is solar energy that was snagged and then transmitted to life via photosynthesis.

Please note that photosynthesis depends on a virtuous cycle. In order for the electrons in plants to absorb solar photons, those electrons have to already be in organic molecules in the plants, most importantly chlorophyll. Only these specific arrangements of atoms and molecules can scoop up solar energy. So here you see the cycle. Plants capture solar photons by using complex organic molecules like chlorophyll, but plants and their chlorophyll need to be built by using solar energy in the first place. It is because of this need for life to be in place, first, in order for life to make itself, that it took our planet so many billions of years of sifting and stirring, all accompanied by *vedanā*, to generate complex photosynthetic organisms. Early primitive cells had to stumble upon photosynthesis. Preexisting, early, less complex life forms had to be present and mutate through unintentional adaptation into the capacity to receive energy directly from the sun, before our current biosphere could effloresce. Our lives are threaded needles, monkeys in mirrors, little twists of fate. We are the lucky efflux from a long cosmic dream.

It is not obvious that life must come into being. Does the universe intend us? Or are we the accidental outcome of a lot of stirring and mixing of a lot of matter, energy, and information over billions of light-years and billions of years of accidental experiments? It is not clear whether biology is a necessary subsequent step to the realm of physics. We don't know whether the complex combinatorial universe of organic molecules that we call life was a mere quirk, a mere happenstance, a one-off event on one planet, or whether, on the contrary, life is driven into being by strong determining forces that spring up repeatedly across many solar systems and many galaxies many times. As we hover among these unanswerable questions from our own perspective, life sounds too complicated to have happened, and yet it is our old, familiar tune. We tend to feel a contradiction. Life sounds improbable and feels inevitable.

*Human* life is a recent addendum to four billion years of organic evolution on Earth, and to fourteen billion years of cosmic evolution. Only seventy million years ago, life was dinosaurs, not people. This very long, very slow creation of us seems to have a lot of weird diversions and useless blind alleys. Was Triceratops really a necessary way-station on the road to humans, Bob Dylan and the Nobel Prizes?

But you and I, we have life, and we move, speak, and think with the energy of our great golden sun. The energy which the sun exudes originally derives from the fusion of hydrogen atoms in the dense, hot center of the sun. The hydrogen fusion that leads to helium and other new elements inside the sun, also creates excess energy called sunlight, or solar photons.

Therefore, all of the energy that plants bring into our biosphere, that becomes our food, that powers our thoughts and emotions, comes from inside hydrogen atoms. We are hydrogen fueled vehicles. Hydrogen indirectly fuels the *vedanā* in our skin or guts. We raise our arms, scratch our ears, and feel sensations with energy of hydrogen atoms broken open.

We owe it to the prophet of science, Einstein, that we know matter and energy are actually different forms of each other. Matter can be converted into the wild energy of atomic bombs. The first energy of the first moments of the universe congealed into matter, predominantly subatomic particles like electrons. It took hundreds of thousands of years before the earliest, small, subatomic particles of matter coalesced into atoms. Atoms are not units, but collections of even smaller things. It was a long wait until atoms themselves replaced subatomic plasma and populated the expanding space of the universe. Most of the visible matter of the universe is still the simplest atom, hydrogen. These hydrogen atoms clump into stars, which are the furnaces that make other, bigger atomic nuclei like helium, iron, carbon, oxygen, uranium, etc. Because matter is actually a form of energy, and because matter consists of subatomic particles, like electrons, which share properties of both matter and energy simultaneously, we can consider that at the deepest level the universe is oscillating matter-energy, the vibration of an infinitely ellusive substrate whose nature remains unknown to us today, hidden inside the mysteries of particle physics, contained by quarks, strings, Higgs Bosons, or other potentially ultimate realities. Scientific experts are probing realities too arcane for our level of language, and understandable only through particle physics and mathematics.

The deepest interpretation of *vedanā*, the sensations of our bodies that we become aware of as we meditate mindfully upon them, is that *vedanā* derive from the wavelets or vibrations of the ultimate matter-energy matrix and flux of the universe. *Vedanā*, or body sensations, may be not only biological, about the movement of atoms and molecules, but also physical, about quantum flux in the depth of things.

A friend of mine, who is a very advanced Vipassana meditator, read my book about wonder, which focuses predominantly upon the transformations of atoms and molecules in the human body. She asked me why I had not referred more to the oscillations of ultimate matter, the vibrations where quantum possibilities allow the finest subatomic particles to emerge from undefinable preexistence, which is allegedly what the Buddha was feeling when he practiced Vipassana to discern the Twelvefold Chain of Causality, and to coin the term, *vedanā*. Those of you who feel the ultimate oscillations of the universe in your bodies as you meditate can now arise and take your seat under the Bodhi tree. For the rest of us, for me, it is more probable that our meditation at best carries us into direct meditative mindful experience of the arising and passing of our octillion fold biological, atomic, molecular matter and energy. The sensations that most of us can feel changing in our bodies as we meditate are caused by the atoms and molecules in our cells, and are unlikely to be subatomic.

## Sensations on the Path to Freedom

Quite probably, for most Vipassana meditators most of the time, the body sensations that we feel arising and passing in almost instantaneous sequence, the vibrating, tingling, unlabelable sensations, are linked to the biological creation and destruction that we embody. We are probably experiencing our sensory nerve endings contacting our skin and generating chemical messengers that bring environmental information back to our brains. We are probably experiencing nociceptors generating chemical messengers to relay information to our brains about the status of our musculature. We are probably experiencing the flow of red cells and plasma through our arteries, arterioles, and capillaries. We are probably experiencing thermoregulators located inside of the hypothalamus of our brain stem changing our temperature up or down by regulating the rate at which we are metabolizing fats and sugars from our bloodstream and our fat cells. There are so many levels and so many transformations that are simultaneously and instantaneously creating and maintaining our temporary aggregate of organic molecules, and it is these that we come in contact with when we meditate upon body sensations, *vedanā*.

Not only our bodies, but our thoughts and feelings, all stir *vedanā*, and therefore as we meditate on *vedanā*, body sensations, we encounter many swirls of emotional storms. Vipassana is not some cool, distanced peering into the universe. Meditation is a dip into the geysers of our being. Every grief or ecstasy we have ever felt is an analogue of roiling aggregates of *vedanā*. Our emotions are embodied in biotransformation throughout our being. We feel our emotions secondary to many molecular changes in our brain, endocrine organs, hearts, guts, even skin.

The subtle sensations that are caused by emotional molecular flows of neurotransmitters and hormones, or the subtle sensations that trigger reactive thoughts and emotions in the meditator who is far from perfect in recognizing all sensations as impermanent, all of the sensations occur in simultaneous, multiple, overlapping, complex and contradictory valences. They are only occasionally uniform and easy to name and interpret. Our body-minds are rich in experiences, memories, problems and promises.

Meditation includes many states of mind such as distraction, daydream, reverie, and reflections. But the goal of meditation is to return to a penetrating realization. If *vedanā* is understood as body sensations, and if *vedanā* is understood as the nexus where craving does or does not occur, then body sensations become the pathway to craving-free, or at least craving-diminished, equanimity. Simultaneously, *vedanā*, or body sensations, become the nexus of the realization of the impermanence of our atomic, molecular, compounded "self." This puts our meditation in line with the Buddha's final summary: that all compounded things are impermanent. Therefore, *vedanā*, understood as body sensations, helps the meditator reduce or cease craving, and attain an equanimity that is coterminus with the realization of *anicca*, the insubstantiality of every formed thing in the universe.

When the meditator is aware of *vedanā*, body sensations, without generating craving or attachment, he or she enters the chain of causal forces that leads to freedom from ignorance about oneself. Awareness of *vedanā* in a neutral, non-commentarial manner was the key step in the Buddha's program to reduce human suffering that was caused by reaction to one's own body sensations. Simple awareness of *vedanā* is the gateway to the Buddha's definition of wisdom.

Finally, I would like to affirm the implication that the universe is not all matter and energy. Non-compounded things, like information, may preexist the universe, or may be intrinsically built into the universe in a non-compounded, non-entropic way. One thought process by which the modern, scientific, meditator, like myself, can consider the Buddha's term, "Dhamma," is to relate it to the scientific laws, the cosmic constraints, that impersonally channel and guide the universal processes that form galaxies and biospheres. Understanding ourselves and everything around us as selflessly insubstantial, while simultaneously vessels of Dhamma, universal law, the information that guides the universe, may be a meditation-derived realization that might reduce suffering in us and in our societies. We are impermanent, but we aren't meaningless. We carry the laws of life and realization inside of us.

Now at last we can look with wonder upon this whole process of observing *vedanā* without reacting. It should be clear that in order for me, or anyone, to feel *vedanā*, and to understand its impermanence, this requires the fourteen billion year long history of the universe, and the four billion year long evolution of life on Earth, by which matter, energy and information cohered temporarily into the process of me, by which life, meaning you and I, could become aware, observational, equanimous and insightful about the fundamental truths of impermanence and lawfulness.

At the juncture of *vedanā*, awareness can become liberating wisdom. At the juncture of *vedanā* an animal on Earth can understand key features of the universe from which we emerged. At the junction of *vedanā*, the universe can become self-realizing.

## Speaking Personally

Speaking personally, the interpretation of *vedanā* as body sensations has given me a focus for meditation that allows me to feel I am a student of the Buddha, without my having to embrace every detail of an organized religion like the various historical Buddhisms. It has allowed me to remain embedded in the biomedical world I studied in my youth, of the electron microscope, the double helix, and the Hubble space telescope, while I walk the path of meditation. Realization of impermanence, and the absence of an enduring self, has given me a modicum of comfort and guidance. My judgements tend to be based upon a bigger perspective. I can balance myself better by seeing my perceived problems in a larger context and in a more radiant light. I can seek out friends among the good and the wise who, according to the Buddha, are the Path itself.

## Vipassana Meditation Centers

Courses of Vipassana meditation in the tradition of Sayagyi U Ba Khin as taught by S. N. Goenka are held regularly in many countries around the world.

Information, worldwide schedules and application forms are available from the Vipassana website.

www.dhamma.org

# ABOUT PARIYATTI

Pariyatti is dedicated to providing affordable access to authentic teachings of the Buddha about the Dhamma theory (*pariyatti*) and practice (*paṭipatti*) of Vipassana meditation. A 501(c)(3) nonprofit charitable organization since 2002, Pariyatti is sustained by contributions from individuals who appreciate and want to share the incalculable value of the Dhamma teachings. We invite you to visit www.pariyatti.org to learn about our programs, services, and ways to support publishing and other undertakings.

## Pariyatti Publishing Imprints

**Vipassana Research Publications** (focus on Vipassana as taught by S.N. Goenka in the tradition of Sayagyi U Ba Khin)

**BPS Pariyatti Editions** (selected titles from the Buddhist Publication Society, copublished by Pariyatti in the Americas)

**Pariyatti Digital Editions** (audio and video titles, including discourses)

**Pariyatti Press** (classic titles returned to print and inspirational writing by contemporary authors)

## Pariyatti enriches the world by
- disseminating the words of the Buddha,
- providing sustenance for the seeker's journey,
- illuminating the meditator's path.

Made in the USA
Coppell, TX
14 April 2021